The Power of Connections

Building Sustainable Relationships

The Power of Connections

Building Sustainable Relationships

E.C. Nakeli

erez
Publishing
Breaking through... Breaking out

Publishing today for tomorrow's generation

© 2012 by E.C. Nakeli

Published by Perez Publishing LLC – *www.perezpublishing.com* –

For your questions and publishing needs write to:
Perez Publishing
548 Congressional Drive
Westminster, MD, 21158
USA
Email: *perezpublishing@gmail.com*
Printed in the United States of America

All rights reserved. No part of this publication may be reproduced, stored in a retrieval system, or transmitted in any form or by any means—for example, electronic, photocopy, recording—without the prior written permission of the publisher. The only exception is brief quotations in printed reviews.

E. C. Nakeli

To contact the author, write to:
E.C. Nakeli
Perez Publishing
548 Congressional Drive
Westminster, MD 21158
USA
Email: *ecnakeli@yahoo.com*

The Power of Connections: Building Sustainable Relationships / E. C. Nakeli

ISBN: 978-0-9850668-0-2

Unless underwise indicated, Scripture references are from THE HOLY BIBLE, NEW INTERNATIONAL VERSION®, NIV® Copyright © 1973, 1978, 1984, 2011 by Biblica, Inc.™ Used by permission. All rights reserved worldwide.

Cover Image: Dreamstime.com, used by permission.

Cover/Interior Design: Zach Essama - *graphicspartner@gmail.com*

Contents

Aknowledgement IX
Dedication XI
Foreword 1 XIII
Foreword 2 XV
Introduction XIX

Part One
The Power of Connections 25

Chapter One
Positive Influences of the Right Connections 27
   1. Uncommon Blessing 27
   2. Uncommon Rescue and Deliverance 29
   3. Uncommon Favor with God 33
   4. Uncommon Favor with Man 34
   5. Uncommon Promotion 36
   6. Uncommon Miracle 38
   Summary of the Chapter 41

Chapter Two
Positive Influences of the Right Connections - 2 43
   1. Uncommon Information 43
   2. Uncommon Restoration 45
   3. Uncommon Solution 47
   4. Uncommon Anointing 50
   5. Uncommon Faith 52
   6. Uncommon Open Doors 55
   7. Uncommon Returns or Results 57
   8. Uncommon Support 59
   9. Uncommon Motivation 62
   10. Uncommon Strength and Resistance 64
   Summary of the Chapter 65

Chapter Three
Negative Influences of Connections 69
   Those Without Connections 70
   The People of Laish 70
   Samson 73
   Summary of the Chapter 77

Chapter Four
The Perils of Wrong Connections 79
   1. Unperceived Blindness 80
   2. Unbalanced Counsel 82
   3. Unnecessary Misfortune 85
   4. Unimaginable Defeat 86

5. Untimely Death..88
Summary of the Chapter 89

Part Two
Building Sustainable Relationships *........................ 93*

Chapter Five
The Mentor/Student Relationship *............................ 95*
    Conviction 96
    Commitment 97
    Corrigibility..99
    Contact and Connectedness 100
    Summary of the Chapter 102

Chapter Six
The Friendship Relationship *.................................. 105*
    1. Mutual Interest...105
    2. Mutual Love...107
    3. Mutual Acceptance......................................109
    4. Mutual Trust 111
    Summary of the Chapter 113

Chapter Seven
A Friendship Kind of Relationship - 2 *.................... 115*
    1. Mutual Transparency 115
    2. Mutual Respect 117
    3. Mutual Identification 119
    Summary of the Chapter 121

Chapter Eight
A Friendship Kind of Relationship – 3 .... **123**
1. Mutual Submission 123
2. Mutual Forgiveness 125
3. Mutual Encouragement 126
4. Mutual Understanding 128
5. Mutual Devotion 130

Summary of the Chapter 132

Chapter Nine
Building Lasting Relationships at the Work Place **137**
1. Be Cognizant of Authority 137
2. Be Conscious of your Duties 139
3. Be Considerate of your Subordinates 141
4. Be Cooperative with Colleagues 142
5. Be Calm in all you do 144

Summary of the Chapter 145

Chapter Ten
Building Lasting Relationships at Home **147**
1. Be Available 147
2. Be Accountable 148
3. Be Responsible 149
4. Be Respectful 150

Summary of the Chapter 151

Aknowledgement

I just want to say thank you to all my friends, children in the Lord, and partners in the ministry for the role each one of you has played consciously and unconsciously in being test grounds for experimenting some of the principles the Lord has taught me over the years on how to build and sustain meaningful relationships. I am where I am today, doing what I do because of my connections to some of you. The power of our connection has lifted and propelled me to where I am today! Some of you I have known for a very long time, others for just a little while but you have each impacted my life to different degrees. I may not be able to mention each of you and what role you have played but let me take a few lines to mention some people specially.

To my beloved parents, Joseph and Comfort Bokwe, thank you for giving me many siblings and so much opportunity to learn how to relate not just with you both but with all of them. Thank you both for the many relatives who lived with us throughout. I learned some of these valuable lessons because you opened our home to so many people.

To my siblings: Vincent, Macaron, Felicia, Maclean, Clovis, Belinda-Jones, and Daphne-Laurel. I say thanks for teaching me the values of relationships as we grew up together.

To my former General Manager, Pastor Jacques Mbang, I say thank you for believing in me and giving me the opportunity to serve in that wonderful financial institution in the role of Branch Manager, and for your understanding and encouragement to me when it was time for me to leave to run with my vision. Thank you, once again, to my wonderful mentors Pastors Simon and Grace Epamba of Christian Missionary Fellowship International, Kumba, Cameroon, you both have been like scaffolds on which I have stood to rise to where I am in the ministry.

Thank you to Pastor Darrell Baer, the conference minister of the Franklin Mennonite Conference.

Thank you, Pastor Robinson and wife Elizabeth Fondong for your tremendous sacrifices.

Thank you, Pastor James and Julienne Ekortah for all your assistance, even when I did not expect.

Thank you to Paul and Adrielle Kempa for your understanding and demonstration of the values of human relationships.

Thank you to my other friends Patrick, Ekole, Rick, Kermit, Emmanuel, Moses, Lotsmart, Enya, Plunkert, the Ngoes, the Marcs. Ours have all been great relationships.

Special thanks go to Lydia for her editorial work. Many blessings!

And finally to my many sons and daughters in the Lord, thank you all for believing in "Daddy Naks" — your daddy always.

Dedication

I wholeheartedly dedicate this book to one special couple whose capacity to relate and sustain relationships has impacted my life remarkably. For a period of about five years they demonstrated almost each one of the principles shared in the second part of this book. From total strangers they became to me like parents and demonstrated acceptance, love, interest, sacrifice, and you name it. Unfortunately they did not live to reap what they sowed in my life during this brief time of knowing them. I am talking of my *"foster"* parents, the late Mr. and Mrs. Daniel and Ophelia Bekondo. Though they are on the other side of glory now, their lives continue to impact me one way or another.

Foreword 1

I believe that you are holding in your hands, a book that will straighten your understanding with regards to sustainable relationships. The value of being connected and benefiting from sustainable relationships cannot be over emphasized. That will be very clear to you as you read through this carefully researched work.

E. C. Nakeli, here presents a comprehensive study on this subject from a biblical point of view. The Lord God our maker has designed us to function in this life as relational beings that are interdependent on one another. Concerning the importance of relationship, we read in Genesis 2: 18, *"And the LORD God said, 'It is not good that man should be alone; I will make him a helper comparable to him.'"*

The success of all achievers in life is to a great extent linked to the quality of the relationships that they have established. When it comes down to the purpose of our life, it will not matter how successful we have been or how many assets we have accumulated. What will be important is that we have built meaningful relationships with people. In fact, a life is wasted if it has not had an impact on the lives of others.

E. C. Nakeli has a strong value for people and he is purposeful and intentional in making relationships a high priority in his life. My prayer is that this book will be used by the Lord to bring healing to ailing relationships and strength to build and maintain sustainable ones. God bless you as you glean from the gems in this study.

>Pastor James Ekor-tah
>Senior Pastor,
>CMFI Riverdale, Maryland

Foreword 2

In every generation the Lord God raises an extraordinary servant, with a unique gift. A prolific writer and author of many books, E. C. Nakeli has distinguished himself as one of those. He has an unusual capacity to expound Scripture. When this Bible teacher writes, whosoever reads, receives divine inspiration. I believe that the impact of his books will soon be legendary. The Power of Connections is one of the best books on the importance of building sustainable relationships I have ever read. I heartily recommend it to anyone who desires to build relationships that will change his or her destiny and advance the Kingdom of God.

The importance of The Power of Connections cannot be overemphasized. We can only ignore it to our own detriment. A man is only as great as his relationships. Who you relate with determines what you will become. Success or failure in life depends on the relationships you build. As long as this message is not a central part of your life, you are bound for failure. From the beginning of life to the end of it, it is who you know and not necessarily what you know that counts. All of creation yearns for the right relationships. Salvation is based on our relationship with God and His Son Jesus Christ. Men will go to hell and be lost forever not only for what they have done, but because they failed to build the right relationship with God and His Son. The power for service in the Kingdom of God depends on our relationship with the Holy Spirit. A happy life, success in business, the Christian life, the marriage life, etc. are based on the relationships we build and maintain. As the author writes:

> When God created man, he did so with the intention and purpose that man's life would be determined both by his relationship vertically with the Triune God, and horizontally with fellow man. In fact, the only thing God said wasn't good was for man to be alone.— Our society will be a million times better than it is today if we all understood and practice the secrets of building sustainable relationships.

Read this book prayerfully and ask the Lord to lead you in the building of the right relationships; your future depends on it. The curse of our generation is the result of a broken relationship with God, broken relationships at home, in the church, in our society at large, and the nations. This book is therefore timeless. A must read for the church and for anyone who desires true success in life. It is the indispensable message of the hour! Fighting in the body of Christ will cease if we would take this prophetic book seriously. I believe God is speaking to the church and we must listen. Much depends on our obedience to what God is saying through our brother, E. C. Nakeli's book. As I told him, I am looking forward to every member of our Church buying a copy. It will change their lives and the life of the church forever.

There is so much to say about this book, but I will end here with this note: history is full of people who succeeded or failed based on their relationships. This is one area you can't afford to fail or take lightly. May God open our eyes to see the importance of this message! Please read and pass it on to anyone who cares to listen.

I thank my friend E. C. Nakeli for this great contribution to the Kingdom of God. It will stand the test of time for many generations to come. When we are gone, our children, and children's children will thank you for this message. May the Lord be glorified in your life and be gracious to you. I love you my dear! Congratulations!!

Rev. Robinson Fondong,
Senior Pastor CMFI Maryland

Introduction

This book stemmed from two messages the Lord led me to preach; the first constituting part one of this book, was preached in my local church where I ministered on the theme, *"The Power of Connections"*. The second part of the book stemmed out of a seminar I ministered in on the theme, *"Building Sustainable Relationships"*. I recall that after the seminar, I was invited to a series of radio shows to teach the subject matter delivered during the seminar. This way the message reached a greater audience and the response was tremendous. Many listeners called in and requested a copy of the message. Unfortunately at the time it was not available in book form. Because of the unusual response the contents of this book brought each time I shared on how to build sustainable relationships or the power of connections, I thought it wise to expand the message and send it out as a book so that many more individuals can be blessed. That is why you are holding this book in your hands at this time.

When God made man, he did so with the intention and purpose that man's life would be determined both by his relationship vertically with the Triune God, and horizontally with fellow man. In fact the only thing God said wasn't good was for man to be alone. It is true that this statement He made was with respect to man's need for a wife. However, it is generally seen that the health and output of man depend greatly on the quality and strength of his relationships. Life is all about relationships! And every normal functional human being yearns for healthy, functional, and fruitful relationships in every sphere of life. It is man's failure to establish and sustain relationships God's way that leads to the anger, frustration, and revenge we find all around us. I have realized that those who have failed repeatedly to establish meaningful relationships often withdraw in disappointment and shut themselves in a world of their own where they open up to spirits of suspicion, hate, depression, and disillusionment. Our society will be a million times better than it is today if we all understood and practiced the secrets to build sustainable relationships. Churches will be livelier and will bring the necessary healing the worshippers seek for if members understood how to build sustainable relationships.

It is not that people do not build relationships or have connections; the problem is whether those relationships can stand the test of adversity and produce meaningful outcomes that can be of benefit to the different parties involved.

The Bible says, *"Unless the LORD builds the house, its builders labor in vain. Unless the LORD watches over the city, the watchmen stand guard in vain."* (Psalm 127:1-2) This tells us that unless we build our relationships God's way, our efforts will amount to nothing. That is why the principles and keys I have shared with you in this book are all based on God's Word and experiences based on and backed by the Word of God. I would not want to share with you human ideas and philosophies; there are already many books out there based on what man thinks would lead to healthy relationships. What I share with you are the things God has prescribed for man to employ as keys to succeed in the building of healthy and fruitful relationships. My prayer for you is that the Lord would grant you understanding and power to employ what has been shared here so that every relationship you build shall be,

> like a man building a house, who dug down deep and laid the foundation on rock. When a flood came, the torrent struck that house but could not shake it, because it was well built. (Luke 6:48)

Part One

The Power of Connections

By connections, I mean our human relationships; the people we interact with, those we know and who know us. Those we hold in one form of esteem or another. Those we can turn to in desperate moments and be sure they are there to answer us.

The first thing I want to say here is that you are where you are today because of your connections of yesterday – those relationships you took time to build and to invest in whether financially, emotionally, socially, spiritually, morally and otherwise. And where you will be tomorrow is determined by your connections today.

The second thing I wish to let you know is that you cannot rise beyond where your connections can lift you. You must understand that human relationships are very pivotal and vital in this pathway to fulfilling your destiny. When God wants to bless and promote a man He does it through our human relationships and when the devil wants to bring a man down he does it through our human relationships. Hence, you see that your connections in life are not neutral. They will make or mar you, promote or demote you, mold or break you.

It is a sad thing that many of God's children think that the only thing that matters in life is their relationship with God. Your relationship with God is foremost and paramount yet not the only relationship you need. Bible history shows that those who made the difference all found favor with God and with man. It is to your own detriment to undermine the importance of human connections. For the purpose of emphasis may I say it again, that God promotes through human relationships. It is for that reason we should be observant and sensitive to God with respect to the people He brings our way, to ensure that we make the most of such opportunities of establishing the right connections.

Your connections are not neutral. They will make you or mar you, mold you or break you, propel you or draw you back depending on the values of those involved.

Permit me to bring to light some very important points, both positive and negative, that will drive home how powerful our human connections are.

Chapter One

Positive Influences of the Right Connections

1. Uncommon Blessing

The right connections with the right kind of people will attract uncommon blessing into your life. One easy way to become blessed is to relate with a blessed man. The anointing for blessing is a transferable anointing which can be transmitted by association. Blessings have the capacity of rubbing over. This is exactly the situation with Lot. Lot the nephew of Abraham had followed him out of Haran to Canaan. The Bible lets us know that God had promised to bless Abraham and we are told that *"Abram had become very wealthy in livestock and in silver and gold"* (Genesis13:2). This was in fulfillment of the promise of God to him. The blessing and prosperity of Abram could, and only could, be attributed to the hand of God on his life. However we are told: *"Now Lot, who was moving about with Abram, also had flocks and herds and tents"* (Genesis 13:5). The only reason while Lot became wealthy was because he was in Abraham's company. His connection to Abraham by association enabled him to tap into the blessing of Abraham. Do you want to be blessed? Keep company with those who are operating under the anointing of blessing. What could have taken Lot a lifetime to achieve, he did in just a short time because of the right kind of connections in life.

Perhaps you are not so sure that it is Lot's association with Abraham that brought about his blessing in his life. To better understand this, follow the drastic turn of events in the life of Lot as soon as he broke away from Abraham. His life went down the drain and he ended up in a cave. Listen to me; there are people you must hold on to in this life no matter what is happening. There are people to whom God has tied your destiny. Breaking from them will mean breaking from the lifeline to fulfilling your destiny. It is your responsibility to be observant of such people and invest in building the required relationship. You want to enter the realm of uncommon blessing and prosperity? Then labor in building and maintaining the right kind of relationships.

A few months ago I received a call from my kid sister over whom I assumed part responsibility for her college education, since my dad went on retirement. I understand the stress that students face especially with all the money needed for personal upkeep and school expenses. Before I left home for the US it was easier for me to meet her needs because I was making a little bit good money. When I went back to school it was no longer possible for me to shoulder this responsibility faithfully. When I received this call she sounded desperate. Now she is a very phlegmatic person in nature and would rather not border anybody. When she called and sounded a bit desperate, I didn't know what to do because at the time I didn't have any money either, and worse still

I was thousands of miles across the Atlantic. She had attempted getting to my parents and for some reasons their phone wouldn't go through. So I appealed to the power of my connections and called a friend of mine back home who is blessed financially, and asked him to send some money to my kid sister, that could sustain her for two weeks before I could send her something myself. To my surprise, he gave her more than four times what I had expected. This was more than enough to carry her through the remaining weeks of the school semester. I connected to his blessing that extended to a sibling of mine because of the investments who've made over the years in our relationship. It should be noted that this same friend of mine, on his own initiative and expense, organized a send forth party for me in their home and invited a good number a people to send me forth when I was about travelling to the US. He recognizes the anointing God has placed over my life and is connecting to it through his financial seeds. My kid sister tapped into his blessings through her connection to me.

2. Uncommon Rescue and Deliverance

Sometimes we get caught in the web of our own folly and wrong decisions. Sometimes we are victims of the circumstances that surround us and find ourselves in helpless situations. There are conditions for which unless help comes from without there is absolutely no way we can free ourselves. At such crucial and critical moments, it will take just the right connections to free us. We need to be connected to those who will be ready to stick their necks out on our behalf. You must constantly evaluate your relationships on the basis of the degree of loyalty. Do you have anybody who can engage themselves in the worst of scenarios to see you free? Is there someone ready to stake it all on your behalf? I am not talking here of a husband or wife or sibling, but one with whom you have nurtured a relationship beyond puny self-interests? I have seen spouses turn their backs on each other in time of need. I have seen siblings care less when they were needed most. The Bible says *"there is a friend who sticks closer than a brother."*

I would like us to stick with the Abraham-Lot relationship for a moment. Because of the increase in their wealth, the land in which they dwelled could no longer contain their livestock and a problem arose between the herdsmen of Abraham and those of Lot. Finally there was an agreement to separate and move in different directions in order to avoid future squabbles. There is one thing I want you to note here; though conflict brought about the separation between Lot and Abraham, they did not separate in conflict. Abraham in his maturity ensured that the parting was peaceful. There comes moments when we must separate in certain relationships. My advice to you is that never separate in animosity. No matter the reason ensure that there is peace before separation. There are people who think that separation must be in conflict and hostility. There are times when business partners can no longer work together, ministry partners might choose to part ways, fiancés might decide to end a longstanding relationship. Whatever it is, let the separation be in peace. The person you are separating from might be the source of your rescue and deliverance in time of need.

For Lot, after his separation from his uncle, the land where he lived was invaded by enemies who overran it and took the inhabitants of the land captive, including Lot. News got to Abraham that Lot had been taken captive. Can you imagine if there was animosity between Abraham and Lot? What would have been Abraham's reaction? But because there was a connection between the two, Abraham engaged himself in a very risky rescue mission that resulted in the deliverance of Lot and the recovery of all that was lost.

> *14* When Abram heard that his relative had been taken captive, he called out the 318 trained men born in his household and went in pursuit as far as Dan. *15* During the night Abram divided his men to attack them and he routed them, pursuing them as far as Hobah, north of Damascus. *16* He recovered all the goods and brought back his relative Lot and his possessions, together with the women and the other people.
> **(Genesis 14:14-16).**

When I was the branch manager of a microfinance bank, there was this young man who was working with us as a collecting agent of our daily savings scheme. He had been with us for over two years under the supervision of my assistant. When I got to check the books for some reason, since I relied on the reports which came from my assistant I normally relied on the information he supplied. However when I decided to do a detailed check of the books I realized this collecting agent had been involved in fraud for a couple of months, unnoticed by his immediate supervisors. My immediate reaction was to have him arrested and prosecuted. All I needed to do was to pick up my phone and call the office of the prosecutor with which I had some connections. Just before then I had realized he was the nephew of a pastor friend of mine. I was perplexed as to what to do; previously I had gotten one other collecting agent jailed for just a little fraud, so my normal reaction was to have this guy jailed. But, what spared him was the fact that he had a connection with someone connected to me. I decided to call his widow mother to my office and explained to her, what had happened and the only reason her son wasn't behind bars. Because of his connections, he was rescued from spending a good portion of his years lamenting in jail. With some arrangements out of court, the family agreed to pay back the money on a monthly basis, which they did. The point I am making here is that sometimes it's not what you know but who you know which will act as a trump card to rescue you from a rather precarious situation, just like Lot was rescued from captivity because of his connection to Abraham.

After ministering in church one Sunday morning; I remember I had ministered deliverance to many people who were bound and the service extended beyond the normal time; I was resting at home in a hot afternoon when I heard the bell to my house ring. When I went to find out who was requiring entrance, it was one of my sons in the Lord. He worshipped in a different center of the same ministry I belong to. When I saw him, he looked very distraught and I knew immediately something was wrong. This young man was an intelligent lad who couldn't pass a high stakes testing that was needed for him to move to the next level as per the academic system of my home country. For some reason, the previous year he had failed, because after answering his questions, a spirit whispered to him that they were all wrong and told him what to write. Needless to say this was not the spirit of the Lord but an evil spirit that was hindering his progress in life. This Sunday afternoon he came to my house for help was the day before he was to sit for this exam for the second time. As he was praying that afternoon the Lord told him to come see me, and so he left everything he was doing and came to my house. Normally because I had ministered deliverance in our center which was the main center, I was tired and wanted to rest. The normal thing I should have done was to schedule a deliverance session for him another day. But his exam was the next day and he needed an emergency deliverance session. Because of his connection to me as a son in the Lord there was nothing I could do but minister to him the very moment. As I laid my hands on his head, he was thrown to the floor by this evil spirit hindering his academic progress. The power of the Holy Ghost came upon me and I commanded the spirit to leave. This captive of a young man was set free. I told him to go write his exams the next day with confidence. When the results came out he was the second on the list in the whole class. The next year he passed the final year high stakes testing without any difficulty because the power that hindered him had been broken. Today he is an engineer in an offshore oil company. What led to his deliverance was his connection to me, so the Lord could ask him to come see me. Even though I was tired and wanted to rest, I ministered to him because of the connection he had with me. There is power in your connections to bring about uncommon deliverance.

3. Uncommon Favor with God

Each one of us is supposed to build a life in favor with God at all times. However this is not always the case as sometimes we find ourselves wanting in terms of favor with God. At such moments our connections may fill the gap where we may be lacking. If we stick with Lot and Abraham here for a moment you will see that Lot got established in a land of perversity and wickedness. The wickedness rose up to heaven and God decided to pour out His judgment on the lands of Sodom and Gomorrah. The Bible says:

> So when God destroyed the cities of the plain, He remembered Abraham, and He brought Lot out of the catastrophe that overthrew the cities where Lot had lived.
>
> (Genesis 19:29)

It was not because of Lot but because of Abraham. God did not remember Lot but Abraham. You need people in your life that will compel God to intervene in your situation in times of crisis.

We do not all have the same level of favor before God. We do not wield the same level of authority in the Kingdom. Some people have found greater favor with God than others. This is what you must understand. We may all be children of God but we do not all have the same authority with God. Sometimes God will spare you from situations not because of you but because of the person willing to make intercession on your behalf. Do you remember Epaphroditus? He was sick and almost died. Paul called him his brother, fellow-worker and fellow-soldier. Yet the reason he was healed and prevented from dying was that God had mercy on him and on Paul. (See Philippians 2:25-30). Just like you need the faith of others to combine with yours for some things to happen, you need the favor others have found with God to combine with the favor you have found for certain things to happen.

4.   Uncommon Favor with Man

Just like you need favor with God to make it successfully through life, so do you need favor with man! The Lord has ordained that man will be the channel of His favor to you. That is why we are told throughout the Bible of people who found favor with both God and man. You need both to rise to your God-ordained heights. Of Samuel, who became Israel's prophet, judge and priest, it is written that *"And the boy Samuel continued to grow in stature and in favor with the Lord and with men"* (1 Samuel 2:26). Of the Lord Jesus it is written that *"And Jesus grew in wisdom and stature, and in favor with God and men"* (Luke 2:52). Could you ever imagine what gave Ruth a Moabite the privilege of becoming an ancestor in the line of the Messiah? It was her connection to Naomi. Her dedication to and love for Naomi led to her being recognized by the people of Bethlehem. Her connection to Naomi gave her favor in the sight of the gleaners in Boaz's field. Because of her connection to Naomi she received the life-changing counsel that led her to get married to Boaz and brought forth the lineage of king David. There are many people today who are married to the right person because of their connections. And there are many others today with wonderful potentials and skills but whom marriage has eluded because of the lack of the right kind of connections. Remember I said when God wants to promote a man He does it through the man's connection or brings you into the right connections. And when the devil wants to destroy a man he does it through the man's connections or brings him into the wrong connections.

When I moved to the US, my plan was to spend a maximum of four months at my friend's place before moving out. Unfortunately, it was difficult to find a job as a student, especially as there was no on-campus job for graduate students in the college I was attending, therefore I couldn't move. My connection to my friend gave me uncommon favor with him such that I could stay in the basement of his house for close to two years without paying any rents or bills. In fact he repeatedly asked me not to make any contributions for the whole time I was there. That is nothing but uncommon favor. When I moved out of his house, another friend of mine offered me his basement for free, no rents, no bills until the end of my program. This is what we call uncommon favor with men. Without such favor I would have been out of school and out of status. Your connections in life are meant to be channels of God's uncommon favor upon your life. Back home I took a young man into my home, who would have been out in the streets. It was my connection to him that made me open my home to him for the period he lived with me before I travelled. Connections release uncommon favor. He had got himself connected to me for mentorship. In fact I brought him up in the Lord when he gave his life to Christ. So in the day of his trouble, he found favor because of his connections.

5. Uncommon Promotion

Why did Esther succeed to rise to the throne as queen? Because of her connections with Mordecai, she was asked to not to reveal her nationality (see Esther 2:10). Her connection to Mordecai gave her favor before Hegai (verse 9) and the favor she found before Hegai led to him unleashing the secret for her to become queen (verses 15 & 17). Sometimes what you need in life are little secrets hidden in the hearts of men who know how to go about things. And favor is the key that opens their hearts and allows them pour out the secrets to you. It is not just what you know but who you know that will open some doors for you in life. Little secrets open mighty doors that launch people into the presence of the great; doors that change you from peasantry to notoriety; from the backdrop of poverty to the limelight of wealth and honor, from obscurity to prominence. Connections in life will reveal to you little secrets which money or intelligence cannot buy. There is untold power in the right connections to bring you uncommon favor before men. And favor will lift you above your peers. It is true that hard work, intelligence, and other skills can lift up a man but these will not do it to the extent that favor would. You need them, but you also need favor above all else. Favor will lift you to high places and give you authority with great men.

When I graduated from college I immediately picked up a teaching job as a high school physics and math teacher. I did that joyfully while serving the Lord as the youth and young adult pastor of my local church. The ministry I am a part of was running a financial institution that had branches in some cities in my home country. There was a plan to open a new branch in my city hence the need for an administrative microfinance bank manager. I had no training in management or accounting and therefore never for one moment thought I could be called upon to assume this responsibility. At the end of one ministers' conference we were having, my senior pastor called me aside and told me of this opening. Some years earlier I had been offered a job which required me to move out of the city. It would have placed me on a higher plain financially and socially than the teaching I was doing at the time. When I considered the fact that it was going to leave me with not as much time to invest in my calling, I was inclined to turn it down, but because of the financial benefit I saw, I was tempted to move. So I decided that whatever my senior pastor will say will be the final decision. After talking with my senior pastor who at the same time is my father in the Lord, he talked to me of the need they had for my ministry, and asked me to stay. It was a hard decision, but I decided to obey. This of course strengthened the bond between us. So when this new opening came, he recommended me for it. He knew of my leadership potentials and integrity with money and so could speak to the CEO of the bank on my behalf. It was not my education (for I was a physicist and not a banker or accountant or finance expert) but my connection that took me from the classroom into an office with a service car. My earlier sacrifice to stay in the city for the sake of the gospel work there was a huge savings in the account of my connection to him. At the right time, it brought about an uncommon promotion in my life. And of course he was not disappointed. By the time I resigned to run with my vision, the CEO of the institution lamented that he was losing his best manager. I produced the results. Your connections will cause others to see the potentials in you which you will otherwise not see. When my senior pastor first told me of the job opening, I turned it down because I thought it was a totally new field for me, and more so because I was to start a new branch from scratch. That was a triple challenge, but with Christ we can do all things!

6. Uncommon Miracle

Somebody is wondering why I have used the expression *"Uncommon Miracle,"* for miracles in themselves are uncommon occurrences. You know miracles do not occur by chance. They happen to those who are in expectation. Now an uncommon miracle is one that occurs even against a person's unbelief. That which happens to a man or woman who does not expect any or believes it can happen to them. Sometimes when you have the right connections in life, the faith of the one you are connected to gives you access into the miraculous, even when you are not expectant of it. The lady in 2 Kings 4:8-17 got herself connected to Elisha by her hospitality and service to the man of God. By making her home open to the itinerant prophet of God she got herself connected to the miraculous. Her sacrifices laid the bedrock for her uncommon miracle. Sometimes you don't need to invest more money into that business; you need to get it connected to the right channel of blessing. If you want uncommon miracles in life, miracles in areas you don't even know require a miracle, then get connected to the right person. After her frequent contact and persistent sacrifices, the day came when the man of God asked what could be done for her. You see sometimes we get disconnected just before our miracle is due. This woman had to persistently provide and sacrifice for the man of God for a long time before she received her uncommon miracle. There are some of you who got connected to the right source of your uncommon miracle but got disconnected just before the miracle flowed. You need to persist. The woman had to turn the visitations of the man of God into a habitation for her uncommon miracle to locate her. It entailed additional sacrifice and patience. When Elisha asked her what she needed she said she had all she needed. She was content even though she had no child. There was a point of need she was not aware of or perhaps she had given up on all hope. Even when her need was pointed out she told the man of God it was not her desire. Sometimes it is the right connections which will open your eyes to a point of need and meet the need. This lady did not believe the servant of God when he prophesied to her but, her connection through her gifts and service to this man linked her to the anointing for breakthrough. She became pregnant and gave birth to a son according to the prophecy. The right connections will resurrect dead dreams and rekindle lost hopes. It did it for the shunammite and it will do it for you. Do you remember the widow at Zarephath? She got connected to Elijah by risking her little food to provide for the man of God and received a constant supply that sustained her and her family through the years of famine. She was ready to eat her last meal and die but she received an uncommon miracle by connecting to the man of God.

While in graduate school, and not having the possibility to work, because my college had on-campus jobs available only to under-graduates; I was faced with the situation where I couldn't have money to pay for my tuition for the next academic year. The money I brought from home was gone by this time and there was the temptation to suspend my semester so I could do some odd jobs to raise money for the next academic year. This would have meant me taking longer to complete a program which was designed for six semesters. I know people who have been in school for several years and have not been able to earn their degree because of financial difficulties. But the Lord God, Jehovah Jireh used my connections to work an uncommon miracle. Through my pastor friend with whom I was living at the time, I was introduced to a group of people who decided to pay a greater portion of my tuition. I didn't ask for it, but because of my connections, someone saw my need and spoke on my behalf to a people I could never have had access to, and a financial miracle was performed. I am leaving graduate school without any school loan. Above all I am completing the program in five semesters instead of the six semesters I was told it was going to take. Your uncommon miracle is awaiting you as you get connected to the right persons in life.

SUMMARY OF THE CHAPTER

- *The anointing for blessing is a transferable anointing which can be transmitted by association.*

- *What could have taken Lot a lifetime to achieve, he did in just a short time because of the right kind of connections in life.*

- *You want to enter the realm of uncommon blessing and prosperity? Then labor in building and maintaining the right kind of relationships.*

- *There comes moments when we must separate in certain relationships. My advice to you is that never separate in animosity. No matter the reason ensure that there is peace before separation.*

- *We do not all have the same level of favor before God. We do not wield the same level of authority in the Kingdom. Some people have found greater favor with God than others.*

- *Sometimes God will spare you from situations not because of you but because of the person willing to make intercession on your behalf.*

- *Remember I said when God wants to promote a man He does it through the man's connection or brings you into the right connections. And when the devil wants to destroy a man he does it through the man's connections or brings him into the wrong connections.*

- *Sometimes what you need in life are little secrets hidden in the hearts of men who know how to go about things. And favor is the key that opens their hearts and allows them pour out the secrets to you.*
- *Connections in life will reveal to you little secrets which money or intelligence cannot buy. There is untold power in the right connections to bring you uncommon favor before men.*
- *Sometimes when you have the right connections in life, the faith of the one you are connected to gives you access into the miraculous, even when you are not expectant of it.*
- *Sometimes you don't need to invest more money into that business; you need to get it connected to the right channel of blessing.*
- *The woman had to turn the visitations of the man of God into a habitation for her uncommon miracle to locate her.*
- *The right connections will resurrect dead dreams and rekindle lost hopes.*

Chapter Two

Positive Influences of the Right Connections - 2

1. Uncommon Information

I mentioned this in passing earlier but let me explain it further so you can understand the power in the right connections to unleash to you the right secrets or information. It is information that formats you for the next level. It is the right secret that secretes the right lubricant for a smooth ride into a new dimension in life. Ask and you will be told that many have avoided loss or made untold profit because they received the right information because of the right connections. The King of Israel escaped defeat from the hands of the Arameans because he constantly received the right information from Elisha. There is power in information to uplift and propel those who properly decode and apply the information. Let us return for a moment to the shunammite. Come with me this time to 2 Kings 8:1-2:

1 Now Elisha had said to the woman whose son he had restored to life, "Go away with your family and stay for a while wherever you can, because the LORD has decreed a famine in the land that will last seven years." *2* The woman proceeded to do as the man of God said. She and her family went away and stayed in the land of the Philistines seven years.

The Lord God had revealed to Elisha the famine which was coming on the land. It was not common information. It was known only to the man of God. Her connection to Elisha gave her access to this information which others did not have. It was personally told her by the man of God because it was not meant to be radio news. This was information that was meant to preserve her from the famine that would hit the land. What was hidden from kings was revealed to her because of the right connections. The information you need to be spared from some calamity may lie with someone you need to connect to. Her family was preserved because of her connection. Sometimes, the only thing that will keep you from the calamity that befalls others is the right information. While others languished in the famine she and her family did not feel a pinch of it. People will not release uncommon information to just anybody. They do it to those to whom they are connected.

When I bought my car and was about to insure it, I was given a ridiculous quote that set me to panic. It was way more than what I could afford at the time because I had had my license for just over a year. I was about to accept the quote when this friend of mine suggested we call a friend to ask him if there was a way we could have a better and affordable quote for the car insurance, at least for liability, for that was all I could purchase at the time. When we made our call, to my greatest surprise, we had a connection that sliced the quote to less than a fifth of what I was charged previously. This was uncommon information I couldn't have had any other way. It saved me a fortune, and is till saving me a fortune. In fact, unexpectedly, this friend of mine took total charge of the insurance bill. There is power in connections to release uncommon information and bring uncommon blessings and prosperity.

2. Uncommon Restoration

Sometimes you find that you have lost everything, or at least the things that count most to you. Many of us seek restoration for things we worked so hard to acquire but which the circumstances of life seem to steal away in the twinkling of an eye. There are many ways in which restoration can come to you. However I do not seek to list them here. I want to talk to you about uncommon restoration, which transcends the normal laws of restoration. I did not say which violates the laws of restoration, but rather which transcends the normal laws of restoration. Some people have to work hard to get their restoration; others tap into the latent power of connections to bring about unprecedented restoration. Sometimes things happen to us for which we might not expect restoration but when we have the right connections it brings about restoration. I want you to stay with me for another moment with the Shunammite. This time let us read our passage in 2 Kings 8 a little further:

> *3* At the end of the seven years she came back from the land of the Philistines and went to appeal to the king for her house and land. *4* The king was talking to Gehazi, the servant of the man of God, and had said, "Tell me about all the great things Elisha has done." *5* Just as Gehazi was telling the king how Elisha had restored the dead to life, the woman whose son Elisha had brought back to life came to appeal

to the king for her house and land. Gehazi said, "This is the woman, my lord the king, and this is her son whom Elisha restored to life." ⁶The king asked the woman about it, and she told him.

Then he assigned an official to her case and said to him, "Give back everything that belonged to her, including all the income from her land from the day she left the country until now."

(2 Kings 8:3-6)

In decoding and acting on the right information given her by the man of God, this lady had left all she had and escaped the famine to dwell in another land. When the famine was over, she decided to return to her country. Now verses 3-6 say she was coming to work her way to restoration. She was coming to beg for her house and land. She saw herself as one who could only beg. And how many people have remained beggars because of the absence of the right kind of connections? There is a level you can operate on which is far higher than begging. You cannot afford to remain a beggar. Ask God for the right connections. Beggars are not only found in streets. There are beggars living in luxury homes and driving posh cars. Too many of God's children are enslaved by the beggar mentality. They beg for what is rightfully theirs. They beg the devil for what has been freely offered them by the finished work on the cross. I deliver you from the beggar's mentality this moment in the name of Jesus.

As this lady came to beg for her land, the latent power of connections gave her a surprise. The Bible says as Gehazi was talking to the king about the exploits of Elisha, this woman who was proof of an uncommon miracle God wrought through Elisha as a result of her connection to him came in to beg for her house and land. When the king talked with her and realized her connection to the man of God he did something incredible. He assigned an official to her case to ensure that she not only receives her house and land but everything that belonged to her before the famine. Not only that, but all the revenue her land had yielded in the past seven years of her absence. Is that not uncommon restoration? Her connections transformed her from a beggar to a dignitary. Her connection gave her access to high places that brought uncommon restoration. There is latent power in connections that will be released at the right time if you keep your connections healthy. Who you are or what you know can potentially limit your accessibility to help in time of need. Who you know can be the trump card that works when all else fails.

3. **Uncommon Solution**

Sometimes we look far for solutions that lie within our reach. Other times we look for solutions which cannot be found unless someone hints us as to where to go. Do you know a man in the Bible called Naaman? He was a commander of the Aramean army, feared, respected and honored even by the king himself. Yet he had a defect called leprosy. It could have handicapped him in the long run had solution not come in time (see 2 Kings 5). Now I have talked a lot about connections and someone has read it and surely misunderstood me to mean connections only with the great. Sometimes your solution will come from obscure, despised and relegated people in the society. That is why in life you should not despise anybody. There are people God brings into your world whom at first sight appear to have nothing you can benefit from but if you listen to your heart or spirit, you will come to terms with the fact that they might hold a key to a door that opens you to new opportunities. Naaman had a problem for which he thought there was no cure. He was ready to go on early retirement and die with his leprosy yet his solution or better still the door to it was with a servant girl. I am sure Naaman was not an approachable man and so the servant girl had to pass through the wife, or was it for ethical reasons? One thing I want you to grasp from here is that be willing to associate and build bonds even with people of a lower echelon in society than you are. The information that brought healing to Naaman was not from fellow generals or people from the king's court, it came from a slave girl who by 'chance' found herself serving Naaman. One thing I give Naaman credit for is his capacity to listen and take advice even from those inferior to him. What set him on the journey to his healing was a suggestion from a slave girl. Even after the prophet told him what to do and he raged and raved and ranted, unwilling to obey because of his status, it was a suggestion from another servant that caused him to obey and consequently receive his healing. Your solution may lie in your connection and willingness to listen to those inferior to you. Uncommon solutions are those which come from sources that will most often than not be despised and neglected, overlooked and undermined. Ask God to open your eyes to behold such vital connections.

When I graduated from college and picked up a job as a high school teacher, I did so with the intention that it was going to be transitional while I sought admission into a graduate program in the USA to continue studying physics. I applied to several graduate programs in the space of two years without any breakthrough. Many of my friends suggested for me to look for admissions elsewhere in South Africa or Europe, but deep within me there was this conviction that the Lord wanted me to be in the US, so I kept trying and finally gave up seeking admissions in the US in 2004. Travelling to America became a dead dream to me at the time. I concentrated on my job and ministry until the Lord began to revive this desire in me once again in 2008. Because I was planning to get into fulltime ministry I decided to apply to a seminary here in the US, and for some inexplicable reasons, my application was denied. Then my solution came from an unexpected source, a connection of mine. My friend Liz knew I had applied to this seminary and was expecting me to obtain the admission. When I didn't, she suggested I could apply to the school she was attending and asked me to have my transcript sent to her. In fact I did not even know the name of her school. Everything just fell into place as the Lord would have it and I was offered admissions into graduate school. This was a solution coming from an unexpected source, it was an uncommon solution. The Lord used my connections to provide a solution to an obstacle which was standing in the way of my dreams. The one question many people have asked me is how I came to choose a small college in a small city in Maryland out of the many schools, cities, and states that are in this country. My response to them has been, *"I had a friend who was attending McDaniel College and recommended her school to me and me to her school"*. God will use your connections to provide uncommon solutions to the obstacles that have stood on your way for a very long time. That is why you should do everything to keep your relations healthy. God uses our healthy relationships to bring blessings into our lives that move us forward in the direction of fulfilling our destinies. Never despise any relationship the Lord brings your way. The day Liz and I got connected more than a decade ago, I would never have imagined that a solution to my dream would come through her. I see you entering the realms of uncommon solution because of the right connections you will establish.

4. Uncommon Anointing

Your connection to an anointed person may give you access into realms of the anointing you will otherwise not attain on your own no matter how hard you work. Connections are channels through which the anointing of the Holy Spirit flows. Throughout scripture you will find people who tapped into the anointing because of their connection to someone who carried the anointing.

Elisha got a double portion of Elijah's anointing not by chance but by design because of his connection to the prophet.

Timothy tapped into the anointing that was on Paul. Because of his connection to Paul, he received gifts by the laying on of hands by Paul.

Joshua connected to the anointing that was on Moses.

The apostles connected to the anointing that was on their Master Jesus.

Nowadays people are connecting to the anointing God has placed on others through networking and fellowships. It is true that many are abusing this. But it is something that works. Remember the devil only fakes what is authentic. I have seen people using it for financial gain and for popularity contests. However, the fact remains that staying connected to an anointed individual gives you access to the anointing. There is latent power in connections to give you access to the anointing of the Sprit. Exploit it! This reminds me of one of my sons in the Lord who committed to wash my car in order to connect to the anointing that he recognized was upon my life.

When I came to Christ, there was this great desire burning in the inside of me to write. I remember I even wrote a tract, though it was never printed. As I read the Bible, I made summary teachings from what I read and studied from the word. I couldn't help but to write. I had papers all over my Bible which contained summaries from my personal Bible reading. I attempted writing books which never went anywhere. My first attempt to write this book you are holding in your hands was back in 2001. The seed of God to write and bless His people was yearning in the inside of me to grow into a tree that will touch lives, but because I lacked the right connections, the anointing that was needed for blossoming was absent until I came into the right connection with a prophet of God by name professor Fomum. On my 24th birthday he happened to be ministering in a crusade in my city, and so I went to him to bless me on my birthday. He laid his hands on me and called forth the gifts of God that was in me. From that day the anointing to write came upon me and I have been writing ever since. In fact I have not been able to keep up with the spirit of revelation that was released from my inside. My connections led to an uncommon anointing. It should be noted that before he went to be with the Lord he had written over one hundred books. There is an anointing that would be released in your life if you will seek the right connections. It could have taken me several years, may be, to activate the gift of God that was in me, but the power of connection did in the split of a few minutes what could have taken some extra hard work to accomplish. You can tap into the anointing through the power of connections. The seed of God that have laid dormant in you will germinate, blossom, and bring forth fruits if you build the right connections.

5. Uncommon Faith

17 One day Jesus was teaching, and Pharisees and teachers of the law were sitting there. They had come from every village of Galilee and from Judea and Jerusalem. And the power of the Lord was with Jesus to heal the sick. *18* Some men came carrying a paralyzed man on a mat and tried to take him into the house to lay him before Jesus. *19* When they could not find a way to do this because of the crowd, they went up on the roof and lowered him on his mat through the tiles into the middle of the crowd, right in front of Jesus.
20 When Jesus saw their faith, he said, "Friend, your sins are forgiven."
(Luke 5:17-20)

Sometimes we find ourselves in situations in which we are really helpless. We cannot do anything to help ourselves even if we wanted to. It is at such a point when all hope is gone that we lose faith or become so weak in faith we fail to hit the minimum threshold faith to trigger divine intervention. At such a moment the power of connections to release uncommon faith is what is needed most. Have you ever realized that when you join faith with your connections, it produces greater results than your faith alone would have ever produced?

Look at this guy who was paralyzed, I don't know for how long. He could have laid where he was and even rotted there if it were not for his connections. Sometimes you might think you are gaining nothing from a particular connection, but at the proper time the latent power of the connection surfaces to be of tremendous help to you. This man's connections when he was whole came to his help when he was paralyzed. The problem with many people is that they build only the kind of friendships or connections that will abandon them when they are paralyzed. When you relate with people on the basis of what you can get from them and not on the basis of what you can give them, you risk being abandoned when you will need them. The one who gives himself out to others will be refreshed in return. Whoever these men who carried him were, it shows he had a living and functional relationship with them. I have seen people abandoned by both the public and near relatives in their time of dire need because they couldn't care less for others when they were in a position to help.

Because this guy was paralyzed, he could not go to the crusade ground by himself but his connections got him there. He could not lift himself up but his connections did. He could not find his way to the place but his connections led him there. When they finally made their way in, the Bible says: *"when Jesus saw their faith..."* It was not just the faith of the man. Most probably his faith was failing like it does for many during very intense trying moments. But it was their combined faith that attracted the Master. Their combined faith had forged a way for them where there seemed to have been no way. It got them not through the human obstacle at the entrance but over it. If these people did not feel what the man felt they couldn't have gone through all this for him. You've got to have connection of people who will feel what you feel, people who can empathize with you. It is difficult for the faith of a man who is separated from your pain to have any positive effect. Sometimes you will need someone or people to stand with you, willing to share in your pain. But such connections are seldom built in times of adversity. Their foundation is laid down in times when all is going well. It is in fair weather that an edifice is raised. But it is very functional in times of adversity. You need such connections my brother/sister and combined faith will make a way where individual faith cannot. Build the right connections and they will work for you when you need them most.

Uncommon faith leads to uncommon breakthroughs! Take a look at Acts 9:36-42 and you will find a woman called Dorcas. She died and the people she had served would not let her go to be with the Lord. In her state of helplessness it was the widows whom she had helped while alive who refused to bury her. They combined their faith on her behalf and decided to send for Peter, who was in a nearby town. The connections she built when she was alive came to her rescue when she was dead. Do not be the kind who will be quickly buried before anything can be done. Establish the right connections and uncommon faith will be your portion when you need it most.

Recently I received a call from my friend whose wife is five months pregnant. For some reason she stopped feeling the heartbeat of the child and called her husband who was out of town, several hours away, to let him know what had happened. Alarmed he asked her to go to the doctor for checkup and when she did; to their disappointment no heart beat was detected. Needless for me to say they both were heartbroken. Now my friend is one of those guys who take nothing lying down. He has such a tremendous faith in God and believes in the prayer of agreement. He called some close friends and asked us to pray with him. Now, my friend believes in my prayers like a little baby believes in its mother. He has always called me to agree with him in prayers whenever there is an emergency or anything for which he needs a joint faith with somebody. I told him I was going to pray for him. We were just about having our devotions in our home. After praying for the wife and baby, I tried calling her so I could pray for her and the baby over the phone, but I couldn't get the call through. It makes a lot of difference when the one you are praying for can hear you pray, especially when making a prayer of command and declaration. I got back to my friend, asked him to call the wife, and instruct her to lay her hand on her womb while as the child's father he called forth the heartbeat of the child. He agreed that he was going to do that immediately. Meanwhile they had transferred her to another hospital just in case. When he got her over the phone and did as suggested, after sometime the heartbeat of the baby returned. He called me a few hours later and spoke from cloud nine. His connections had brought about an uncommon faith that brought life back into a fetus. The connections you have will determine the miracles you experience in life, and some miracles require uncommon faith for them to take place. And the shortest cut to the realm of uncommon faith is your connections.

6. Uncommon Open Doors

> *15*Simon Peter and another disciple were following Jesus. Because this disciple was known to the high priest, he went with Jesus into the high priest's courtyard, *16* but Peter had to wait outside at the door. The other disciple, who was known to the high priest, came back, spoke to the servant girl on duty there and brought Peter in.
> (John 18:15-16)

Have you seen people make their way through but they reach critical points and cannot progress any further because they do not have the right key to the doors that matter? Few people have access to everywhere, if at all any. Sometimes you need someone to refer you for the door to be opened. You need someone to commend you to move to the next level. You need someone to hold your hand and say to the gatekeepers, "*this one has to go in*". There are places where your voice is not recognized, places where what you say does not matter. At such a time, you need the voice of someone who is known. There are doors that what you know or who you are will never open yet will open readily if one who matters in that circle stands with you. Have you seen people who have prayed and prayed for something and nothing happens? It is because their voice is not recognized in the domain where their solution is held in the spirit realm. The door you have been knocking at all this while which has remained closed to you will open if you build the right connections. Listen, even in heaven's courts we do not all have the same authority with the King. We do not all have the ability to open doors, let alone every door. Remember that Peter had been given the key to open doors, but this door into the courts of the high priest was closed to him. It was John who came and spoke with the gatekeeper and enabled Peter to get in. Peter's connection to John opened the right door for him. Sometimes your prayers may not open the door you need, but with your connections as a bolster, they will. Sometimes your proclamations will not open some doors but they will in combination with your connections. Mind you that you are not relying on the connections. You rely on God alone but He will use your connections to open the doors for you.

I travelled to our capital city back home to meet with the late professor Fomum, without prior arrangement to meet him. Now, this was a very busy man with a tight schedule. It was not easy to see him even upon appointment. Then one day a young man in the name of E. C. Nakeli came to see him without having booked an appointment in advance. When some people asked me why I was in Yaoundé, I told them the reason and some told me it would be impossible to see him. I was told even those who pray with him do not find it easy to meet him out of the prayer meeting. I thought I had wasted my time and money to travel for over 200 miles for a visit that was going to be abortive. It happened that my spiritual mother was in Yaoundé at the same time I was visiting. She was the one who held my hand and took me into his office immediately after the prayer night was over. In fact someone had hinted me that the best way to see him was to stay at the prayer night. Later I was able to talk with him while he was having breakfast at home, again due to the influence of my spiritual mother. When it was time for me to leave back to the province, many people were surprised that I had that easy access to see the man of God. What created this open door that many had predicted was going to be closed to me was my connection to someone who had access into the presence of the servant of God. Who you know will open doors for you that will surprise many.

7. Uncommon Returns or Results

Two are better than one, because they have a good return for their labor.
(Ecclesiastes 4:9)

The power to produce uncommon results lies in connections. What you can accomplish alone is no match to what is accomplished when you create the right connections. The business world understands this. That is why you see mergers here and there. Companies merge to boost profit. This is a Bible principle from which the world is benefiting but to which the Church seems to be blinded. One will have a return but two will have a good return. This means that the combined benefit even when separated will be more than what one would have gotten.

Remember the Lord told the Israelites that one of them will chase a thousand and two of them will chase ten thousand. Therefore connections will produce quintuple results, to the least. You can multiply your results five times if you get the right connections. You can rise to five times where you are now if only you can establish the right connections. A tremendous power to multiply is embedded in the right connections. The wise tap into it. The foolish go solo.

Many of us will accomplish much more than we are now doing if we tapped into the latent power locked up in connections. The dream to own a publishing company was birthed in me from above more than a decade ago. I have been handling it in prayer, fasting and careful planning, invested time and money in research for years on how to go about this. However, I understood that at a certain point I will need to tap into the unlimited power in partnership. So I decided to partner with some of my trusted connections to establish this company, having invested many years of research and laying of the ground work. I prayed that the Lord will bring just the right partners into this venture that will spread the word across the nations and help fulfill the dreams of many young authors. Through this partnership with my connections, we were able to raise the funds needed to get Perez Publishing on the move. Now we are unstoppable, the throne is the limit to where we will rise, and the ends of the earth are the limits of our influence. The fact that you are holding this book in your hand is a sign of a successful partnership through the connections God brings into our lives. Instead of just one visionary, we are a team of visionaries looking into the distant future with eyes of eagles. Surely if I was still trying to do it alone it could have taken me several months to have this going. My friend, tap into the unlimited power of partnership!

8. Uncommon Support

9 Two are better than one,
because they have a good return for their labor:
10 If either of them falls down,
one can help the other up.
But pity anyone who falls
and has no one to help them up.

(Ecclesiastes 4:9-10)

You can only be supported as far as the connections you have established. No matter how strong you are, sometimes you need external support to survive. I am not talking here of the unhealthy dependence on others but of the vital sustenance that connections produce. Jonathan had his armor bearer to give him support when he went against the Philistines. David had Jonathan to lend him emotional support and encouragement when he came under the attack of Saul. Paul could not work in an open door because he couldn't find Titus. Peter had John with whom he could go to the Temple to pray at the time of prayer. Jesus sent His disciples out in pairs. Those who understand that support comes from connection reap the benefit and those who despise it are ruined by their ignorance and arrogance.

There is no one who was as anointed as Samson in the Old Testament. But no one else fell beyond recovery like he did. This is because he had no connections, hence no one to watch his back. Many people hold that Samson's problem was immorality but that is only the secondary issue. The primary cause of Samson's failure was that he had no support. Look at all his accomplishments and you will see what I am saying. For other judges at the time it is said that so and so rallied men behind them and went to battle. But for Samson, it was always, *"... and Samson went against the philistines…"* no matter how anointed you think you are, there are things your anointing will not do for you. It cannot take the place of others in your life. You need someone to tell you that that relationship is becoming inappropriate. You need someone to remind you that you are leaving the realm of faith into the realm of presumption. You need someone to remind you of the principles that guide your work and walk. You need someone to remind you of the boundaries you must observe in your walk and work. Someone to tell you brother it is time for us to pray or study the word rather than watch TV. There is tremendous power in connections to keep you on track and provide the necessary support when you need it most.

I was ministering in a conference organized by one of my minister friends to celebrate the anniversary of his ministry. I was scheduled to speak twice, Thursday evening as the first speaker and Friday morning as the only speaker. I couldn't attend the rest of the conference because I had to minister on Friday and Saturday evenings of that same weekend in a crusade my church was organizing. During this brief time at the conference I had met casually one other minister who was the second speaker on Thursday night of that conference and we somehow had exchanged contacts though we never got in touch until when he was in great need for support. He was trying to start a church in our city, and the other ministers he had programmed to speak at his conference disappointed him at the very last minute for reasons I would not mention here. He had just one speaker and himself to minister in this program and so he didn't know what to do since the conference was scheduled for three days. In his desperation he turned to me for help and asked if I could come support his program by ministering. As bank manager I had a very busy schedule coupled with my responsibilities to my local church. But one thing is that I have a heart for the work of the Lord to see it grow independent of who through whom God is working. I accepted to support him in this program and went and rendered ministry. He succeeded to start an assembly and I believe the church is doing well. What gave him the uncommon support he needed is his connection to me. If we had not established that connection when we first met, he would have been left stranded at a time he needed support. God will bring people your way whom you may need in the unforeseen future. Do not despise any opportunity to establish connections and build relationships.

When I was to graduate from high school, I had told my dad I wasn't going to go to college immediately. I told him I wanted to work for some time and save some money with which I could travel abroad. My intention was to travel to Germany to study. So I bought some books that were to help me teach myself German. I also received tutorship from some acquaintances. I invested time and was making some progress in my study of German. Then one day my friend's mom asked me of my plans about college and I told her what I had decided to do. Because throughout the year I had been tutoring my friend, who was her son, in the sciences, she told me I was too intelligent to take that risk of not going to college. She told me I risked ending up in the job I was going to get and advised me to do everything to go to college. Remember I had told my dad it was not my plan to go to college immediately upon graduation. With a few weeks left on the deadline to get registered, I went to my dad to inform him of my change of plans. Needless for me to tell you the response was negative. He told me college was no longer in his immediate agenda for me and therefore there was no money allocated for that. When I told my friend's mom of what was going on, she offered to pay my first year college fee. In fact we both went to the bank and she paid the money into the university account. That was an uncommon provision for me to go to college that came as a result of my connections. I had invested time in tutoring her son and this was a plus in the account of my connection to her. Of course my mom sold one of her property that helped paid for my rents and other expenses in that first year and beyond. By the time I was leaving for college, my dad had changed his mind and had come on board. But the uncommon provision that set me on the path to college education came as a result of a connection. Who knows, the story of my life could have been different. You wouldn't be reading this book now because it was during my first year in college that God got hold of me and changed my life for His glory. I had spent seven long years running from God after my initial encounter with Him when I was in seventh grade. There is latent power hidden in connections, it set me on the right path to fulfilling my destiny, and made uncommon provision!

9. Uncommon Motivation

> Also, if two lie down together, they will keep warm.
> But how can one keep warm alone?
> (Ecclesiastes 4:11)

There are moments when you find no intrinsic motivation to pursue a cause. Such times you can tap into the power of connections to keep you motivated. Warmth in the above passage can mean motivation. The steam you need to keep riding that path sometimes will come from those to whom you are connected. Sometimes you can motivate yourself but that does not work every time. People have given up because they found no one to pat their backs when they needed it. Sometimes in the midst of fierce opposition you may need someone to help you stir the course.

Sometimes with depleted resources you need a word of hope from someone you are connected to. Build the right connections and remain motivated.

One of my greatest weaknesses as a believer was the inability to take extended complete fasts. For several years in the Lord I was only able to go for two days complete fasts, though I had them frequently, for my personal spiritual growth. When I moved to the city of Kumba after graduation, I found myself connected and praying with this group of elderly women. I loved to be with those who invested time in prayer. These ladies were all fasting machines. Long extended fasts were a normal routine for them. It was easy to see them fast for up to forty days while drinking only water and taking some vitamins. It was not long before their motivation to fast rubbed over and I fasted for three days complete for the first time in my life. As time went on, I fasted for seven days in a row and my motivation to fast continually improved as I rubbed shoulders with these fasting machines. Then, there came the time I went solo on a twenty-one day complete fast encouraged by these giants. This was one of those turning points in my spiritual walk. Now, though thousands of miles away I can take longer fasts because my connections to them had motivated me to the level where I was no longer afraid to fast for prolonged periods. The people you connect yourself to will determine what you are motivated to do and how motivated you are in life. I do not need for corporate long fasts to be proclaimed before I undertake one; the motivation I received is still stirring me on for exploits.

10. Uncommon Strength and Resistance

Though one may be overpowered,
two can defend themselves.
A cord of three strands is not quickly broken.
(Ecclesiastes 4:12).

There is power in numbers. And there is power in knowing that there is someone or there are some people willing to lend you support at any time you may need it. Sometimes just knowing someone is there for you galvanizes and energizes you in areas where you will otherwise be considered a weakling. Building the right connections is one way to ensure that you are strong. You can be emotionally stronger when you are connected to the right persons who lend you emotional support. You can be professionally stronger when you are connected to the right persons who lend you professional support. Take whatever domain you can, it will make you stronger by being connected to the right persons.

SUMMARY OF THE CHAPTER

* *It is information that formats you for the next level. It is the right secret that secretes the right lubricant for a smooth ride into a new dimension in life.*
* *There is power in information to uplift and propel those who properly decode and apply the information.*
* *What was hidden from kings was revealed to her because of the right connections.*
* *Some people have to work hard to get their restoration; others tap into the latent power of connections to bring about unprecedented restoration.*
* *Her connections transformed her from a beggar to a dignitary. Her connection gave her access to high places that brought uncommon restoration.*
* *Sometimes your solution will come from obscure, despised and relegated people in the society.*
* *There are people God brings into your world whom at first sight appear to have nothing you can benefit from but if you listen to your heart or spirit, you will come to terms with the fact that they might hold a key to a door that opens you to new levels.*
* *One thing I give Naaman credit for is his capacity to listen and take advice even from those inferior to him.*

- *Uncommon solutions are those which come from sources that will most often than not be despised and neglected, overlooked and undermined.*
- *Your connection to an anointed person may give you access into realms of the anointing you will otherwise not attain on your own no matter how hard you work.*
- *There is latent power in connections to give you access to the anointing of the Sprit. Exploit it!*
- *When you relate with people on the basis of what you can get from them and not on the basis of what you can give them, you risk being abandoned when you will need them.*
- *You've got to have connection of people who will feel what you feel, people who can empathize with you.*
- *The connections she built when she was alive came to her rescue when she was dead.*
- *You need someone to hold your hand and say to the gatekeepers, "this one has to go in".*
- *Have you seen people who have prayed and prayed for something and nothing happens? It is because their voice is not recognized in the domain where their solution is held in the spirit realm.*
- *What you can accomplish alone is no match to what is accomplished when you create the right connections.*

- *You can multiply your results five times if you get the right connections. You can rise to five times where you are now if only you can establish the right connections.*
- *No matter how strong you are you need external support to survive sometimes.*
- *Those who understand that support comes from connections reap the benefit and those who despise it are ruined by their ignorance and arrogance.*
- *You need someone to remind you of the boundaries you must observe in your walk and work.*
- *People have given up because they found no one to pat their backs when they needed it.*
- *Sometimes just knowing someone is there for you galvanizes and energizes you in areas where you will otherwise be considered a weakling.*

Chapter Three

Negative Influences of Connections

We said before that when God wants to promote a man, He does it through the man's connections and when the devil wants to destroy a man he does it through the man's connections. As much as there are positive influences of connections, there are also negative influences. The wrong connections in a man's life can ruin him permanently. That is why the wise are very cautious in establishing connections of any kind. There are two sets of people vulnerable to the negative influences of connections; those who have the wrong kind of connections and those who do not bother to establish appropriate connections. Let us examine both categories:

Those Without Connections

There are too many people living their lives in total isolation and unhealthy independence. Such people are living in a self-sufficient world without any regard for the right kind of friendships. They have established invisible but very perceptible barriers to keep others out of their lives. The closest person to them knows nothing at all about their secret world. In fact this state of being is far more dangerous than of those who have the wrong kind of connections. I'll like us to take a look at two case studies in the Bible of people who had no connections.

The People of Laish

I'd like us to take a detailed look at Judges 18 so that you can have a better idea of what we are going to say in this section. I will be citing only the verses that we deem essential to drive home the point we are to make here. Verse 7 of the passage says:

> So the five men left and came to Laish, where they saw that the people were living in safety, like the Sidonians, unsuspecting and secure. And since their land lacked nothing, they were prosperous. Also they lived a long way from the Sidonians and had no relationship with anyone else.

Like these Laishists, there are many people living in the apparent safety of their own little world from which everyone else is shut out. Invisible but very obvious and insurmountable barriers have been erected all around them such that anyone who dares to access their world is met with utmost resistance. For many, the simple reason is their self-sufficiency. They live in affluence and do not deem it necessary to relate with anyone. Such people view every potential relationship as a threat to their wealth and security. The people of Laish lacked nothing. They lived in prosperity. The Bible says their closest neighbors who were the sidonians lived a long way from them. Are there not many people out there who befit this description? Their closest neighbors or closest relationships are dealt with at arms length. There is nobody who really knows them or who can readily respond in times of emergency. Many live like strangers to the very people they live with in the same home or neighborhood. Haven't you heard of people who have committed suicide to the surprise of many? Such people lived in the midst of others without establishing the vital links or connections that sustain people and offer hope in difficult circumstances. Loneliness is not the absence of people in your environment but the absence of vital connections with the people around you. In this Western world driven by competition, greed, insecurity, and betrayal, people are afraid to open up their lives and let others into their world. Hence many live behind the bars of disguised self-sufficiency. When God made man He placed in man the innate desire for healthy relationships and vital connections. God's principle of connections is ingrained throughout creation but man seems to have found a way to bypass the need for connections. It is for this reason we find wrecked lives clothed in tuxedos and driving expensive cars. To deal with this void, many have turned to drugs and other harmful behaviors with animals and objects.

What is it about the people of Laish that made them live in isolation from others and hence vulnerable to attack and defeat to the Danites? Let me group the reasons in three categories as stated in the passage:

- A false sense of security: *"so the five men came to Laish, where the people were living in safety…, unsuspecting and secure.* (verse 7a)
- A false sense of self-sufficiency: *"And since their land lacked nothing, they were prosperous."* (Verse 7b)
- A social disconnect: *"Also, they lived a long way from the Sidonians and had no relationship with anyone else."* (Verse 7c)

In our contemporary world, and it's a shame to say even in Christendom, many people build their lives on such faulty and unstable ground as the Laishists only to discover when it's too late that their false sense of security and sufficiency has betrayed them in the face of adversity.

In every society, there are Danites on the loose looking for culprits to take advantage of. It is our vital connections to those around us that will help us stand and defend ourselves in case of attacks. Look around you and you will find the Danites of suicide. Check again and take note of the Danite called depression, together with her twin brother frustration. Turn to the left and find their kinsmen called loneliness, discouragement, despair, disillusionment, and disappointment. These are the spies that make the reconnaissance and rally the whole tribe of invaders to destroy lives that lack vital connections to people who are meant to act as pillars of their lives. Listen, there are some relationships you just can't do without. The reason the Lord Jesus saved you and made you a part in His body is so that you may build the vital connections which are meant to hold and sustain you when things are good and when they are bad. I am not saying your life should depend on people. Jesus Christ should be the center and foundation of your life. But there are people He has placed around you to whom you must connect in order to accomplish your purpose and fulfill your destiny. The response you get when you cry for help is proportionate to the relationships you have established in the course of your daily life. The opportunities and possibilities that you see before you at any one time in life may be tied to the connections you have established in life. Life is all about relationships, and relationships cost a deal of time, devotion, finances, emotions, and determination to build. It is the cost of building vital and sustainable relationships that make people shy away from it. Anything of worth requires time and commitment. In our world today, people lack the power and ability to commit to others. Even when commitment is present, it is shallow and superficial to stand the test of time and adversity.

When the Danites arrived at Laish, the Bible says, *"they attacked them with the sword and burned down their city. There was no-one to rescue them because they lived a long way from Sidon and had no relationship with anyone else"* (see VV 27 & 28). Life is relationships. Christianity is all about the right relationships. To overlook the importance of vital connections for your life is to forfeit the blessings and privileges that come with them.

We have looked at a community of people who lacked the vital connections and how this led to their destruction. Now I want us to take a look at an individual whose destiny was destroyed because he failed to establish the right connections and partnerships for life.

Samson

As I studied the life of Samson, his exploits and the reason why he failed, I realized he did fail because of the lack of vital relationships. Each time Samson went on any mission, he did it alone. The only time he is said to have gone somewhere with his parents was when he was using them to accomplish his selfish ends. There are many people like that who see the need for others only when they will serve their selfish purposes and interests. Everything he did was done alone. As I looked closer into the pages that hold his narrative, I discovered that Samson was a very secretive person. When he killed a lion, he did not even let his parents know he had killed a lion. When he got honey from the carcass of the lion and gave some to his parents he never told them where the honey came from. And to my disappointment his parents did not even bother to ask him where he got his honey. If Samson was a little open to the people around him, he would have let his parents know where the honey came from and they in turn would have reminded him of the rules of his life. After coming in contact with the carcass, he needed to have purified and re-consecrated himself as a Nazarene. Samson's downfalll did not begin with Delilah, it started from his desecration of the Nazarene vow. There are many people dying in the secretiveness of their lives, meanwhile just opening up to the right person will save them from death and destruction.

I read about a prophet who died a debtor (see 2 Kings 4). This man was so secretive his wife did not know he was in debt. Even his mentor Elisha did not know this guy was in debt. He was so secretive that he died under the pressure of his debts and problems. If I may ask you, is there anyone in your life who knows you in and out? Is there anyone who knows your victories and defeats, and your successes and failures? Is there anyone who knows your inner fears and pressures? This man had a connection to his solution but he failed to make use of it because of secretiveness. There is no way Elisha would have known this guy was in debt and not performed a miracle to help him out. Do not allow the pressures of life to kill you while you bleed gradually in your secret corner. God placed you in His body so you can find help in times of distress. Do not allow secretiveness to send you to an early grave like it did the prophet. He was in the company of prophets but failed to build the right connections. No doubt he died young! When he died creditors began pouring in to ask for their money. I am quite sure the wife was taken aback by the number of people coming to ask for their money. She realized she never really knew the man she had lived with for so many years. When everything was gone and there was nothing more to be sold, one of the creditors came for the children of the man, in particular they came for his sons. This means the children were still very young for the creditor to be able to cease them from their mother. Hey woman, it is time you asked your husband where the documents of the house are. Ask him where the car documents are and where other important documents of the family assets are. Let him show you where they are before anything happens and the banks come for the house, and you find that you have nowhere to lay your head. Your solution lies in the environment God has placed you in. Build vital connections by being vulnerable. There can be no solid relationships without vulnerability. Life is all about taking necessary risks.

Let's get back to our man in focus here, Samson. Like I said before, he was a man who lacked vital connections as a result of unhealthy secretiveness. He went on his missions alone and did everything of his alone. In spite of all his anointing he ended up a miserable man. Read his story in Judges 13-16 and you will see for yourself that this guy lacked vital connections. Throughout you will read *"and Samson went against the philistines…"* He was a one-man army; no doubt he fell so easily. Listen to me my brothers and sisters. No matter how anointed you are, no matter how intelligent and hardworking you are, no matter how gifted and talented you are, no matter how spiritual you are, you need somebody to watch your back. You need somebody to tell you when you are crossing the line. You need someone who can remind you of your vows and Christian responsibilities. You need someone on whose shoulders you can cry when things are not going and all you need do is cry. I wish I could say it more clearly and emphatically. But I remember I was told "*a word to a wise is sufficient*".

Throughout this book I have emphasized the importance of vital relations and how to build them. We have seen how the lack of such vital connections can be detrimental to the destiny of a group of people, families, and individuals. Now there is another part I want us to get into. Just as the right relationships or connections will make a man's destiny, so the wrong relationships and connections will mar his destiny. Thus in trying to establish vital connections, we must beware of what wrong connections can do. In the following pages, I would like us to examine some situations.

SUMMARY OF THE CHAPTER

- *There are too many people living their lives in total isolation and unhealthy independence.*
- *Loneliness is not the absence of people in your environment but the absence of vital connections with the people around you.*
- *When God made man He placed in man the innate desire for healthy relationships and vital connections.*
- *In every society, there are Danites on the loose looking for culprits to take advantage of. It is our vital connections to those around us which will help us stand and defend ourselves in case of attacks.*
- *The reason the Lord Jesus saved you and made you a part in His body is so that you may build the vital connections which are meant to hold and sustain you when things are good and when they are bad.*
- *The response you get when you cry for help is proportionate to the relationships you have established in the course of your daily life.*
- *Life is all about relationships, and relationships cost a deal of time, devotion, finances, emotions, and determination to build.*
- *To overlook the importance of vital connections for your life is to forfeit the blessings and privileges that come with them.*

- *There are many people dying in the secretiveness of their lives, meanwhile just opening up to the right person will save them from death and destruction.*
- *Do not allow the pressures of life to kill you while you bleed gradually in your secret corner.*
- *Build vital connections by being vulnerable. There can be no solid relationships without vulnerability. Life is all about taking necessary risks.*
- *No matter how anointed you are, no matter how intelligent and hardworking you are, no matter how gifted and talented you are, no matter how spiritually strong you are, you need somebody to watch your back.*
- *Just as the right relationships or connections will make a man's destiny, so the wrong relationships and connections will mar his destiny.*

Chapter Four

The Perils of Wrong Connections

I said earlier that no connection (relationship) is neutral in itself. Our relationships are making or marring us consciously or unconsciously. The connections you are involved in will promote or demote you, bring you direction or confusion, and make you fulfill or miss your destiny. We examined the benefits of the right connections in the earlier part of this book. We did look at the dangers of staying without connections in the last section. Now I want us to take a look at the dangers or perils of the wrong connections. When satan wants to bring a man down, he gets him involved in the wrong connections. I have understood that just as God reaches men through other men; to uplift, promote, and establish; so does the devil reach men through other men; to demote, drag, and destroy. The people you allow in your inner circle in particular or those you relate with in general have the potential to pull you down. Wisdom is the capacity to build the right kind of relationship; it is also the capacity to keep away from the wrong relationships. Many lives have been wrecked because at some point in time, they let their guard down with respect to whom they allow into their lives. Below are some ways in which wrong relationships allowed can be a peril.

1. Unperceived Blindness

The greatest blindness is that which the victim is unaware of. It is one thing to be blind and aware of your blindness and totally another thing to be blind and unaware of it. For a moment I want to take you back to our story between Lot and Abraham in Genesis 13. When God called Abraham to leave his people and his country to the land He was to show him, Abraham left but took Lot along. As long as Lot was with Abraham, there was no way he could see that which God had for him. The name Lot means a covering, a veil. Lot was the veil that blinded Abraham from seeing into the future. Because God wanted to fulfill His purposes for Abraham and the world He orchestrated a scenario that brought about their separation. Listen friend, there are some relationships, some people who are veils to the vision God has for our lives. As long as we cling and hold on to such we deprive ourselves of the great things God has in store for us. You must constantly evaluate your relationships on the basis of their impact on your destiny and theirs as well. Any relationship which is not contributing to the fulfillment of God's purpose of at least one party involved is not worth it. Have you ever taken time to ask yourself who the veils in your life are? The sad thing is that many people have so many veils in their lives that they have become accustomed to. Their vision is permanently shrouded. Until there is a radical separation and breaking away from such relationships vision will continue to be illusive for them. Every Lot needs to go. Take a look at this:

> *14* The LORD said to Abram after Lot had parted from him, "Look around from where you are, to the north and south, to the east and west. *15* All the land that you see I will give to you and your offspring[a] forever. *16* I will make your offspring like the dust of the earth, so that if anyone could count the dust, then your offspring could be counted. *17* Go, walk through the length and breadth of the land, for I am giving it to you." *18* So Abram went to live near the great trees of Mamre at Hebron, where he pitched his tents. There he built an altar to the LORD.
>
> (Genesis 13:14-18)

God had wanted to talk to Abraham and show him his future, but there was a veil in the life of Abraham. Immediately the veil was taken off God could now show him what He wanted to.

"The Lord said to Abram after Lot had parted from him...." With the removal of the veil comes revelation and empowerment. Every covering is a block to divine destiny. May the Lord open your eyes to identify the relationships that are a covering or are blocking the sunshine of destiny from reaching the garden of your life! May He also grant you the courage to part with your beloved Lots! You may have become attached to them. You may suffer some bleeding heartaches because of their departure but it's worth you seeing God's vision for your life. Nothing is worth separating you from God's divine purpose and calling upon your life. I want you to know that you can be blessed but blind. Abraham was blessed and had great wealth but wasn't able to see into that which the Father had in store until the vital separation. I see you taking the bold step of separation. I see your eyes opening to God's vision.

I see your ears hearing divine direction. I see you moving into the highway of accomplishment of your vision. By the power of the Holy Spirit, I command every veil of blindness to be torn from your life in the Name of the Lord Jesus. I command the scales to fall off and never return in Jesus Name.

2. Unbalanced Counsel

The counsels you receive and respond to in the course of your life determine who you become, what you achieve, and what you miss out in life. Many lives have been wrecked because of one wrong piece of counsel. Counsels come with associations; associations suggest connections. The wrong connections will bring us the wrong counsel which ultimately wrecks lives. We find a vivid example of what wrong counsel can do in the case of Rehoboam, son of Solomon. After inheriting the throne of his father Solomon, the people brought a request to the king who was wise to seek counsel. Let's look at the passage. 1Kings 12:1-14 :

> *1* Rehoboam went to Shechem, for all Israel had gone there to make him king. *2* When Jeroboam son of Nebat heard this (he was still in Egypt, where he had fled from King Solomon), he returned from[a] Egypt. *3* So they sent for Jeroboam, and he and the whole assembly of Israel went to Rehoboam and said to him: *4* "Your father put a heavy yoke on us, but now lighten the harsh labor and the heavy yoke he put on us, and we will serve you."
> *5* Rehoboam answered, "Go away for three days and then come back to me." So the people went away.
> *6* Then King Rehoboam consulted the elders who had served his father Solomon during his lifetime. "How would you advise me to answer these people?" he asked.

7 They replied, "If today you will be a servant to these people and serve them and give them a favorable answer, they will always be your servants."

8 But Rehoboam rejected the advice the elders gave him and consulted the young men who had grown up with him and were serving him. *9* He asked them, "What is your advice? How should we answer these people who say to me, 'Lighten the yoke your father put on us'?"

10 The young men who had grown up with him replied, "These people have said to you, 'Your father put a heavy yoke on us, but make our yoke lighter.' Now tell them, 'My little finger is thicker than my father's waist. *11* My father laid on you a heavy yoke; I will make it even heavier. My father scourged you with whips; I will scourge you with scorpions.'"

12 Three days later Jeroboam and all the people returned to Rehoboam, as the king had said, "Come back to me in three days." *13* The king answered the people harshly. Rejecting the advice given him by the elders, *14* he followed the advice of the young men and said, "My father made your yoke heavy; I will make it even heavier. My father scourged you with whips; I will scourge you with scorpions."

Notice that when Rehoboam sought the counsel of the elders, he dissociated himself from them by asking the question, *"how would you advice me...."* However when he got to the youths he asked, *"How should we answer this people?"* thereby associating himself with the younger people. It is therefore not questionable why he readily bought the counsel of his age mates and rejected the wise counsel of the elders. Only fools surround themselves with those who think like them and act like them. There is no wisdom in surrounding yourself with a set of clones. Another thing I want to tell you is that there are relationships which we outgrow.

Sticking to a relationship that is no longer relevant is the shortest cut to demotion. You have to seek new counselors as you progress in life. If you are moving ahead in life, some people who may have been your good and trusted counselors yesterday may not qualify to be your counselors today. A person can only give you counsel as far as he knows how to. The sad thing is that very few people who pose as counselors are honest enough to say it is time for you to move on to another person who can give you the right counsel you need at this level in your life. Therefore it is your responsibility to reevaluate your counselors with respect to what they have to offer to you at your new position or stage in life. I wish I could say it in a more emphatic manner. Evaluating your relationships with respect to what you have to offer or receive is very vital. There are people to whom you were very important yesterday, but to whom you are not as relevant today. Wisdom demands that you move ahead to where you can be of maximum influence. Many people get frustrated in life because they hold on to relationships they must let go. They hold on to counselors whose counsel is no longer relevant for their success. This is what led to the downfall of Rehoboam. Unbalanced counsel is more dangerous than wrong medication. I should not be misunderstood here to mean people should not stick to relationships; it will violate everything I will say in part two of this book. What I am saying is that you must know which relationships are necessary for you to maintain for a lifetime. There are people who are meant to be pillars in your life and you can't afford to part with them for whatever reason. Yet there are some relationships which are only relevant for a season. That is why Solomon said, *"There is a time for everything, a season for every activity under heaven; … a time to embrace and a time to refrain…a time to keep and a time to throw away."* (Ecclesiastes 3:1, 5b, & 6b). Keeping that which you are supposed to throw away will cause it to stink and bring discomfort. Are there some relationships you are holding on to which you are supposed to have thrown away? May be that is why all you get from them is discomfort. Think again.

3. Unnecessary Misfortune

Misfortune will come in one way or another but there are some which are unnecessary. Some people owe the misfortunes in their lives to the wrong kind of connections. Whether in business, ministry, or whatever sphere in life we may consider, those we are connected to will bring in their input be it positive or negative, consciously or unconsciously. I would like us to look at a case study in the Bible which depicts the importance for people, believers especially, to consider whom they associate with especially in business. Turn with me to *2 Chronicles 20:35-37*, where we find Jehoshaphat king of Judah, a very godly king, prosperous in every venture he undertook. However at some point in time he made an alliance with Ahaziah king of Israel who was basically a demon worshipper. His association and business alliance with this ungodly king brought about the failure of his business. As believers, we should be cautious as to who we covenant with in business. Covenanting with people who have other covenants links us indirectly to their covenants, thus exposing whatever we do under the banner of that covenant to satanic attack. There are moments God will lead you to do business even with those who are not His servants. I believe it is near impossible to do business only with those who are in the faith. However, we should be certain that God is leading us, especially in situations where we have to form partnerships with the other parties. The only reason for the failure of these business ventures of Jehoshaphat was his association and alliance with the wicked king. There are very vital inquiries you've got to make when getting into any kind of alliance. Find out the source of the person's contribution into the business; would it stand before the law of the land governing the business? Would it stand before the standards of God? What or who does the person worship? Will he keep your business separate from the worship of his god or will he take the business before his god? Such questions are essential to keep us from the pull of huge capital. Many people have lost huge sums of money because they got involved, rather unwittingly with those whose source of capital is questionable. After many years of hard work and great expectations they come to the bitter truth of the fact that they have built on very shaky ground. You can prevent loss by examining the lives of those you get into an alliance with, whether in business, ministry or otherwise.

4. Unimaginable Defeat

Life is full of battles we face consciously and unconsciously. Sometimes we meet with defeat which we cannot explain and wonder what on earth is happening to us. We tell ourselves we have been at our best, given all we could, employed all we know yet came out battered, shattered, splattered with debris, and hampered by the battles of life. It is true that we all face defeat, at least temporarily, in one area of our lives or another. Such defeats are necessary to make us strong and ready for further battles. They drive us to total dependence on the Lord. However, there are defeats which can be totally avoided; they come to us because of our associations. It is important to know and consider the people you ally yourself with to face the battles of life. Some associations make you vulnerable to defeat in some areas of your life. A vivid illustration of this fact can be seen in the passage of 2 Chronicles 25:5-10. Amaziah, king of Judah was going to war. He decided to hire some troops from Ephraim to add to his already large army in order to face the enemy with the power of numbers. But God was not pleased with his choice of association and sent a prophet to warn him of his wrong association, telling him it will guarantee his defeat. The men of Ephraim instead of being of help like he thought, , would instead make him vulnerable to defeat. You must understand that the people you take into battle will determine whether you are a winner or a loser. The people you pray with will determine whether your prayers are answered or not. That is why the King of kings often chose discretely, those He prayed with depending on the situation at hand. There are certain prayer topics you just can't afford to pray with some people.

Paul exhorted Timothy to *"fight the good fight of faith."* That exhortation is for you and me too. To be effective in this fight you have to choose your fighting comrades with wisdom. Endeavor to know their standing before God. Are the people walking with God? Will they provide a landing spot for the enemy or provide a bridge in the wall of defense? These are very vital questions you must ask yourself before enlisting support from whomever in the battles of this life. You can avoid unnecessary defeat by choosing wisely. This will demand you take before the Lord, everybody in your camp and ask Him to reveal to you their actual state. You cannot win in the fight of faith if there are Achans in your ranks. God will give you the wisdom to deal with the Achans and the backslidden people of Ephraim of your life, as seen in our passage above.

5. Untimely Death

The graveyards are filled with lives which were cut short before they could even begin realizing their God-ordained dreams. Most often the cause of such untimely deaths can be traced to the wrong connections and bonds. Jehoram, a young man who took over the throne of his father Jehoshaphat after he went to be with the Lord; abandoned the ways of the Lord and walked in wickedness because of his connection to the house of Ahab. Under their influence he sold himself to do evil (see 2 Chronicles 21). It was not very long before God passed a sentence on him through the mouth of His prophet. Watch who you associate with! May you not die before your time because of the wrong connections! May the Lord guide you in the choice of your friends and associates!

SUMMARY OF THE CHAPTER

* *Our relationships are making or marring us consciously or unconsciously. The connections you are involved in will promote or demote you, bring you direction or confusion, and make you fulfill or miss your destiny.*

* *There are some relationships, some people who are veils to the vision God has for our lives. As long as we cling and hold on to such we deprive ourselves of the great things God has in store for us.*

* *With the removal of the veil comes revelation and empowerment. Every covering is a block to divine destiny.*

* *Nothing is worth separating you from God's divine purpose and calling upon your life.*

* *Only fools surround themselves with those who think like them and act like them. There is no wisdom in surrounding yourself with a set of clones.*

* *If you are moving ahead in life, some people who may have been your good and trusted counselors yesterday may not qualify to be your counselors today.*

* *There are people to whom you were very important yesterday, but to whom you are not as relevant today.*

- *Many people get frustrated in life because they hold on to relationships they must let go. They hold on to counselors whose counsel is no longer relevant for their success.*

- *There are people who are meant to be pillars in your life and you can't afford to part with them for whatever reason. Yet there are some relationships which are only relevant for a season.*

- *Some people owe the misfortunes in their lives to the wrong kind of connections.*

- *Covenanting with people who have other covenants links us indirectly with their covenants, thus exposing whatever we do under the banner of that covenant to satanic attack.*

- *It is important to know and consider the people you ally yourself with to face the battles of life. Some associations make you vulnerable to defeat in some areas of your life.*

- *The graveyards are filled with lives which were cut short before they could even begin realizing their God-ordained dreams. Most often the cause of such untimely death can be traced to the wrong connections and bonds.*

Part Two

Building Sustainable Relationships

A relationship is said to be sustainable if it can be maintained and preserved over time. A sustainable relationship is one which can stand the test of time and adverse circumstances without a weakening in its strength and output.

In this section we are going to look at sustainable relationships at two levels:

- That between a disciple maker and the disciple or teacher and student or master and servant or a mentor and mentee.
- That between friends, mates, spouses, siblings, colleagues etc.

In any relationship, you must be able to define the category to which it belongs so as to apply the right virtues. If you mix them up then problems will automatically arise and there will be a weakening in both the strength and the output of the relationship.

For any relationship to be sustained, there must be a purpose for that relationship and it will vary with relationships and with people. Every relationship has some common goals and values, whether short or long term, shared by the parties involved. These common goals and values may be clear or unclear, known or unknown, hidden or secret; whatever the case may be.

Chapter Five

The Mentor/Student Relationship

I want to present to you four distinct qualities that must be involved for there to be a successful and sustainable mentor/student relationship. The sad thing is that we are in a generation where young people are plagued with two major syndromes: presumptuousness and the Rehoboam spirit.

By presumptuousness, I mean the *"know it all"* attitude that many people carry today. That is one of the major problems in society today. Young people today are antagonistic to learning and guidance. It is this unwillingness to learn that has resulted in the destruction of many lives. There are many mature people today available to guide the young, were they willing and humble to listen. Many great destinies will be fulfilled if only the young were open to counsel.

When I talk of the Rehoboam spirit, I mean the tendency for young people to reject mature counsel, shun the company of the mature or elderly, thereby spending all of their time together and receive unwise and immature counsel from each other. Any young person who must succeed in life must treat himself of these syndromes.

For a sustainable mentor-student relationship, the student must understand that your mentor is not your friend. There may be friendship in the relationship but it is never based on the principle of friendship even if you were age mates or your mentor is younger than you. If you treat it as a friendship something becomes lost from the relationship.

The four indispensable qualities are:

✿ Conviction

> *14* At this they wept again. Then Orpah kissed her mother-in-law good-by, but Ruth clung to her.
> *15* "Look," said Naomi, "your sister-in-law is going back to her people and her gods. Go back with her."
> (Ruth 1:14 -15)

You must be convinced first of all of what you want in that relationship and secondly you must be convinced that the person in question is capable of helping you achieve it.

If you must build this kind of sustainable relationship your choice must not depend on popular opinion and on the attitude of others but on your personal conviction. Ruth's relationship with Naomi was based on her conviction if not she would have followed Orpah to return when Naomi urged her to do so. Why many a mentor/student relationship does not last is because people get into it without knowing what they want and without being convinced that the person in question is able to help them achieve their dreams. If you know what you want you will insist on having it in spite of the weaknesses and failures of the one from whom you are learning. There is power in conviction to keep you sticking to somebody for tutorship when all others see nothing good coming out of it. Popular opinion will not keep you going when things become tough between you and your mentor. Do not get into it because some other person has gotten into it otherwise you will soon get out of it because some other person has gotten out of it.

Conviction is so vital to the sustention of such a relationship. In 1 Kings 19:19-21, the Bible says after God asked Elijah to go anoint and commission Elisha, Elijah went and threw his cloak around Elisha. When Elisha wanted to follow Elijah, the man of God spoke harshly to him and asked him to go back. Surely, Elisha by this time had realized that his destiny was tied to Elijah. He was convinced that Elijah was the man he had to follow. And His conviction led to him returning to follow Elijah who apparently did not want him to go along. You need conviction for your relationship with your mentor or mentee to last. This will cause you to hold on to the relationship even during difficult and uncertain times. Be convinced that you have a role to play in your mentee's life or that your mentor has something to offer you which you may not obtain anywhere else. Conviction carries with it the power to sustain.

☙ Commitment

16 But Ruth replied, «Don't urge me to leave you or to turn back from you. Where you go I will go, and where you stay I will stay. Your people will be my people and your God my

God. *17* Where you die I will die, and there I will be buried. May the LORD deal with me, be it ever so severely, if anything but death separates you and me.
(Ruth 1:16 -17)

Those whom God has given to us as mentors are not perfect people. They too have their own weaknesses, of which God was fully aware before He ever arranged for us to be mentored by them. Ruth did not bother about the weaknesses of Naomi or her people. She was committed to going with Naomi wherever she went, to staying with her wherever she stayed, eating what she ate, living or dying with her. This is total commitment. She even bound herself by oath to Naomi. God does not and will never reward superficiality. For your relationship to be sustained it needs a total heart's commitment from the student to his teacher. It is this kind of commitment that Timothy and Titus had to the apostle Paul. Thus they were able to stand with him through it all. John Mark at the beginning did not have this kind of commitment though he later developed it. Demas never developed this kind of commitment and at a certain point he deserted his master when he was needed most.

There are many young people today moving from one person to another seeking mentorship. This should not be the case. Their problem is that of lack of commitment. Nothing ever works without commitment on the part of those involved. One serious aspect of commitment is determination to go the whole way. You must be determined to go the whole way with your mentor if you must become a person of substance. If you return with me to the story of Elijah and Elisha you will again see the aspect of commitment involved in this mentor-mentee relationship. When it was time for Elijah to be taken to heaven (see 2 Kings 2:1-18), we see that though he urged Elisha to go home and spare himself the trouble of following him all over, Elisha decided to stick with his master wherever he went. He faced not only the discouragement that came from his master but that which came from the company of the prophets. It was his commitment to his master that caused him to overcome these obstacles. Listen to the words of Elisha to his master: *"As surely as the Lord lives and as you live, I will not leave you."* (2 Kings 2:2b). This is a commitment that comes from the heart. It was like Elisha was taking an oath never to depart from his master. It is this kind of commitment we need in order for the mentor-mentee relationship to produce befitting results for all involved.

ஐ Corrigibility

By being corrigible, I mean the capacity to accept correction, reprimand and if need be punishment without taking offence. Many people today are not corrigible. When you correct them they become angry and withdrawn. There are many who do not want to be rebuked or reprimanded. To build a sustainable mentor/student relationship, the student must accept or submit to reprimand and punishment if need be without taking offence. The Bible says so in 1 Timothy 3:16-17:

> [16] All Scripture is God-breathed and is useful for teaching, rebuking, correcting and training in righteousness, [17] so that the man of God may be thoroughly equipped for every good work.

Look at Peter for example in Matthew 16:23: *"Jesus turned and said to Peter, "Get behind me, Satan! You are a stumbling block to me; you do not have in mind the things of God, but the things of men."* The Lord Jesus used such harsh words of rebuke that for many today, it would have sent them packing their bags never to return again for discipleship. Rebuke and correction are tools in the hands of your mentor to cut off and trim the rough edges from your life. They are means to preserve and protect you from error. There must be somebody whose *"no"* is final in your life. If not you are heading for destruction. And how many lives have been destroyed because of incorrigibility. Do not be one who is only interested in those who praise and encourage all the time. Stick to those who can discipline you. This will increase your efficiency and efficaciousness. The first step to a downfall is to decide to run away from those who can correct you and stick to those who flatter you. It is a route that leads to nothing but a fatal crash.

Let us take a look at another relationship between a mentor and a mentee that illustrates this point of corrigibility. Moses was in the wilderness with the children of Israel, administering justice to them. His approach to leadership at the time was not very effective. We know that Moses was a man who talked with God face to face, yet he allowed himself to be corrected by another human being. In Exodus 18, we see Jethro rebuking Moses for his approach and counselling him on how to get things done. We are not told that Moses went and sought the Lord about it. He accepted correction from his mentor. Be open to correction, regardless of your anointing and wisdom. God will send people your way to save your ministry, business or life by providing you with necessary corrections.

෩ Contact and Connectedness

When I talk of contact here, I mean the aspect of being available. You must be able to be reached at any time by your mentor.

- ✴ There must be physical contact through your services.
- ✴ There must be psychological contact through your gifts in case you are far away.
- ✴ There must be spiritual contact through your prayers.

Stay connected to your mentor even in your attitude. This will go a long way to make your relationship a success.

Connectedness here is not limited to physical or communicational connection. You need to stay connected in values and way of life. You need to be connected in spirit. Paul mentioned the fact that when Titus visited the Church in Corinth, he acted in the same spirit as he (Paul) would have acted. This means Titus was connected to his mentor (See 2 Corinthians 12:17-18). Unlike Titus we see that Gehazi was not connected to his mentor. That is why even with the rod of his master he could not perform the miracle of raising the dead boy to life. He was always around his master but he was not connected. His disconnection from the spirit, values and ways of his master was exposed when he ran after Naaman for profit even when his master had asked Naaman to go with all he had brought. If Gehazi was connected in spirit to his master, he would have acted in line with him (See 2 Kings 5).

SUMMARY OF THE CHAPTER

- *We are in a generation where young people are plagued with two major syndromes: presumptuousness and the Rehoboam spirit.*

- *Many great destinies will be fulfilled if only the young were open to counsel.*

- *You must be convinced first of all of what you want in that relationship and secondly you must be convinced that the person in question is capable of helping you achieve it.*

- *Popular opinion will not keep you going when things become tough between you and your mentor.*

- *God does not and will never reward superficiality.*

- *To build a sustainable mentor/student relationship, the student must accept to be rebuked and punished if need be without taking offence.*

- *Rebuke and correction are tools in the hands of your mentor to cut off and trim the rough edges from your life. They are means to preserve and protect you from error.*

- *The first step to a downfall is to decide to run away from those who can correct you and stick to those who flatter you. It is a route that leads to nothing but a fatal crash.*

- *We are not told that Moses went and sought the Lord about it. He accepted correction from his mentor.*
- *You need to stay connected in values and way of life. You need to be connected in spirit.*
- *If Gehazi was connected in spirit to his master, he would have acted in line with him.*

The Friendship Relationship

Many people today lack the capacity to build lasting friendships; they change their friends seasonally like trees shedding their leaves. The main reason behind this is not that their goals are changing but it is the absence of virtues that sustain a relationship. Let us look at the twelve distinct qualities that sustain any relationship belonging to this class:

1. Mutual Interest

> Each of you should look not only to your own interests, but also to the interests of others.
>
> (Philippians 2:4)

You must be genuinely interested in each other. You must show some interest in each other's goals and dreams. You must show mutual interest in each other's welfare. When this is lacking the relationship cannot be sustained even if one party is interested. Everybody wants to hang around and stay close and intimate with those who show interest in their person and in what they do. You see it is one thing to be interested in somebody, another thing to be interested in what the person is doing and in the output of the person. Many people limit their interest only in what the other is doing and this gets hampered when the results are not forth coming. It is good to be interested in what someone is doing but a lot better when you are interested in the person as a whole. When you are interested in a person as a whole you will be patient when the person is not up to par with respect to results or output. Let me give this example. In the local church where I fellowshipped back home, there is this choreography group made up of some youths, both male and female. When they started the group, their first performance was so thrilling that others later joined the group. Now in a crusade after some weeks, the group was to perform and there was this young man who had joined the group. They had already mounted the stage and were in a posture to begin when one of the matrons requested that this young man be sent off the stage because he may not have mastered his role. Sitting beside the lady and hearing it all, I humbly told her what I thought, that it was neither the right time nor place to correct the lad. I knew it would probably deeply affect him mentally and emotionally. She however insisted that he might make mistakes and finally he was sent off the stage. After the program, of course he was battered and shattered and never again went to the training sessions. What am I trying to bring out by narrating this story? You see the matron was more interested in the dance output than in the well being of the lad. If she had by any means been interested in him, then she would have allowed him. If he had not mastered the dance well, the stage was not the right place for him to have been sent away. That should have been taken care of in a more dignified way that would have caused no wounds and left no scars. In every relationship, if it must last you should be interested in the person primarily before being interested in what they are doing. Show interest in the goals and dreams of the person. People will cling to those who help them realize their goals and dreams. Look for means and ways to be part of what the other person is doing. This will give the other person confidence and courage that he or she is secure in what he or she is doing. There must be mutual interest. Asking about their wellbeing is an appropriate way to demonstrate interest. Ask questions like: how are you doing today?, How was school?, Hope work is coming up great?, How is your walk with God? These may be ordinary everyday questions but when asked in a tone of sincere concern, they will minister life and health to our relationships.

2. Mutual Love

> We ought always to thank God for you, brothers, and rightly so, because your faith is growing more and more, and the love every one of you has for each other is increasing.
> (2 Thessalonians 1:3)

> This is my command: Love each other.
> (John 15:17)

You must love each other and demonstrate the love. Let the person know that you love him or her. It is not a weakness to love somebody even if that person is of the opposite sex. You see the sad thing in our society today is that the devil has succeeded to corrupt and convert this notion of love to mean sexual love or feelings and people are afraid to show their love for others especially for members of the opposite gender. Love is what binds everything together (Colossians 3:14); when it is lacking all artificial cords will soon give way and things will fall apart.

No matter how strong one sided love is, it can never compare to mutual love. The Lord Jesus exhorted us to love one another with the same love He loved us. Such love shapes our outlook and enhances our output. Every human being yearns to be loved. There are few who really do want to give out love. If your relationship must last, you must love each other, though it can never be to the same degree. For no two persons can love mutually to the same degree. But for things to work well, the love must at least attain a level where it can be described as strong. Another thing is that a man can only give out what he has. And none of us has love in himself. True and lasting love comes only from God. In order to love, you should open yourself and receive love from the source of love which is God through Jesus Christ. When you allow the love of God to fill your heart, you can then let it flow to others and be a blessing. Love is one of those rare virtues that will last forever. A relationship based on love has a strong foundation, and will outlive little squabbles and misgivings that would otherwise have strained and broken it. To better understand the importance of love, Paul's first letter to the church in Corinth explains the characteristics of love. Paul's definition of love is the yardstick of our commitment to one another. Assess your level of love by meditating on these; identify the area where you are lacking and make necessary adjustments.

Also the Bible makes it clear that hidden love is virtually useless. There is no need to hide the intensity of your love for a person, or worse still, keep it a secret altogether. David and Jonathan loved each other very deeply. It is that profound love that kept their relationship thriving through the heart of turmoil. David maintained the relationship long after the death of Jonathan by helping his descendants. His posthumous loyalty to Jonathan was born out of that special bond of love they both shared. Love will sustain your relationship from collapsing in the face of the fiercest ordeal.

3. Mutual Acceptance

1 Accept him whose faith is weak, without passing judgment on disputable matters. *2* One man's faith allows him to eat everything, but another man, whose faith is weak, eats only vegetables. *3* The man who eats everything must not look down on him who does not, and the man who does not eat everything must not condemn the man who does, for God has accepted him. *4* Who are you to judge someone else's servant? To his own master he stands or falls. And he will stand, for the Lord is able to make him stand.
5 One man considers one day more sacred than another; another man considers every day alike. Each one should be fully convinced in his own mind. *6* He who regards one day as special, does so to the Lord. He who eats meat, eats to the Lord, for he gives thanks to God; and he who abstains, does so to the Lord and gives thanks to God. *7* For none of us lives to himself alone and none of us dies to himself alone. *8* If we live, we live to the Lord; and if we die, we die to the Lord. So, whether we live or die, we belong to the Lord.
(Romans 14:1-8)

You must be willing to accept each other the way they are. This is the most difficult thing to do because as humans there is always the tendency to want others to conform to your desired image of them. However unless you accept a person without trying to change them, the relationship cannot be sustained. When you accept someone as they are, it is much easier for you to change and adapt to accommodate him/her. Everybody wants to stay where they are accepted. Did you know that the most difficult thing to do is to try to change somebody and the easiest thing to do is to change yourself? However, we tend to take on the more challenging task in this case. There are some people who do not build any lasting relationship because they want to relate to perfect people. Of course the so called perfect standards they set are with respect to their own values. If you must build a lasting relationship, you must learn to accept people for who they are and for what they are without attempting to change them. It is God alone, in the power of the Holy Spirit who can change an individual. So the best you can do is pray and not impose. Where there is mutual acceptance, there is room to accommodate each other's failures and weaknesses. Even in cases where those involved are born again, no one is yet perfect. If you are the kind who always does things speedily, in order to relate well with someone who does things slowly, you may have to reduce your speed. By doing this you will be making room for the slow nature of the other, otherwise the relationship will be strained and eventually break apart. Paul said we should make room for the weaknesses of others and therefore accept them. It might be character weaknesses, temperamental weaknesses, or even moral weaknesses. Once you have accepted the person, you may then take the necessary precautions in order not to be affected negatively by that person's weaknesses. If you have a friend who has a problem with money for instance, accepting the person's weakness might mean never lending money to that person, so that your relationship is not strained. In such a case if you are to give him or her money, you certainly are not expecting any repayment. Mutual acceptance is necessary and indispensable for any sustainable relationship. Like the hymn writer who said, *"Take me as I am"*, you will learn to tell each other *"I accept you as you are."*

4. Mutual Trust

> It always protects, always trusts, always hopes, always perseveres.
> (1 Corinthians 13:7)

This is another vital element for the building of any lasting relationship. There is nothing that destroys a relationship like suspicion. Suspicion or lack of trust strains and strangles a relationship if it is not dealt with. Trust repels suspicion. You cannot suspect someone you trust. If there is any question in your mind with regards to the behaviour of a person, it is always better to ask questions and get to the truth, rather than build your own conclusions. When you trust someone, you feel secure around the person and when someone knows that you trust him or her, he or she will also feel a sense of freedom and security in your presence. The person will be free to share his/her goals and dreams with you. The person will be open to share his/her fears and even his/her weaknesses with you. It is true that absolute trust is to be placed in God alone. However there is a degree of trust that needs to exist in our human relationships. Trust will boost your confidence when you are dealing with the person. Confidence is an important factor that sustains relationship. I know there are countless stories of trust that have been betrayed, and as an after effect such people find it difficult to trust anybody. If you are a child of God and are sensitive to the Holy Spirit, He will guide you as to who you can trust and in case of misguided trust, He will quickly call your attention. The truth is there are always sign posts in a person's life that indicate whether such a person can be trusted with something or not. There are people whom you can trust with money but not with your wife or daughter. There are others you can trust with your wife or daughter but who cannot be trusted with a dime. It is your responsibility to identify if the person is trustworthy. You need to apply wisdom and develop personal methods and tests for different areas of trust. This aspect of trust is closely related to that of understanding your friend or whoever it is you are relating with. We shall look at mutual understanding later. But for now let's look at another element which is interlinked with trust; it is the aspect of transparency.

SUMMARY OF THE CHAPTER

- *Everybody wants to hang around and stay close and intimate with those who show interest in their person and in what they do.*
- *People will cling to those who help them realize their goals and dreams. Look for means and ways to be part of what the other person is doing.*
- *These may be ordinary everyday questions but when asked in a tone of sincere concern, they will minister life and health to our relationships.*
- *Love is what binds everything together (Colossians 3:14); when it is lacking all artificial cords will soon give way and things will fall apart.*
- *None of us has love in himself. True and lasting love comes only from God. In order to love, you should open yourself and receive love from the source of love which is God through Jesus Christ.*
- *A relationship based on love has a strong foundation, and will outlive little squabbles and misgivings that would otherwise have strained and broken it.*
- *There is no need to hide the intensity of your love for a person, or worse still, keep it a secret altogether.*
- *Unless you accept a person without trying to change them, the relationship cannot be sustained.*

- *There are some people who do not build any lasting relationship because they want to relate to perfect people.*
- *It is God alone, in the power of the Holy Spirit who can change an individual.*
- *Suspicion or lack of trust strains and strangles a relationship if it is not dealt with.*
- *When you trust someone, you feel secure around the person and when someone knows that you trust him or her, he or she will also feel a sense of freedom and security in your presence.*
- *There are people whom you can trust with money but not with your wife or daughter. There are others you can trust with your wife or daughter but who cannot be trusted with a dime.*

A Friendship Kind of Relationship – 2

1. Mutual Transparency

6 If we claim to have fellowship with him yet walk in the darkness, we lie and do not live by the truth. *7* But if we walk in the light, as he is in the light, we have fellowship with one another, and the blood of Jesus, his Son, purifies us from all sin.
(1John 1:6 -7)

8 For you were once darkness, but now you are light in the Lord. Live as children of light *9* (for the fruit of the light consists in all goodness, righteousness and truth) *10* and find out what pleases the Lord. *11* Have nothing to do with the fruitless deeds of darkness, but rather expose them. *12* For it is shameful even to mention what the disobedient do in secret. *13* But everything exposed by the light becomes visible, **14** for it is light that makes everything visible. This is why it is said:

Wake up, O sleeper,
rise from the dead,
and Christ will shine on you.

(Ephesians 5:8 -14)

Hypocrisy (duplicity) is what causes most relationships to get broken. For a relationship to be sustained, the parties involved must be transparent with each other. By transparency, I mean the capacity to be open to each other about your failures and weaknesses. Let the other person know what you think about him or her. Never give the other a wrong opinion about yourself or of what you think of him or her. Be open and honest. As children of light we must walk in the light. Personally I hate and detest dealing with people who have double personalities because it is the devil's nature. There is healing power locked up in transparency. When you are open one to the other, wounds will easily be healed. Hurts will be dealt with appropriately. It is difficult to harbour a grudge against someone you are open to because you will always let him or her know how you feel. What breeds unforgiveness is the lack of openness! Transparency will cut the ground from under any tendency of distrust or suspicion. Misgivings about the actions of someone will block the flow of love. But when you are open one to another, you will not be afraid to ask the necessary questions to the person concerned in order to clear your mind of any doubts. When you allow doubt to accumulate because you do not ask the right questions, it will definitely insulate and isolate you from each other, thereby weakening the relationship. Remember fellowship is the life of any relationship. If there is no fellowship because of insulation and isolation, the relationship cannot be sustained.

Transparency will mean you telling the other where it hurts and why! It will mean letting the other know your position about a particular thing without fear of being rejected. Transparency will mean telling the other party what you think about his actions and attitudes before drawing any conclusions. It is the strength of any relationship which must stand the tests of time and adversity. Transparency breeds trust and enlivens confidence. Transparency is the very opposite of duplicity. Any relationship built on a false impression comes to an abrupt end when the hypocrite is discovered. Even if it does not end abruptly it will inevitable suffer a fatal blow from which it might never recover, but for a supernatural intervention. That thing you cannot let the other know about you is not healthy for any relationship. It is a cankerworm that will gnaw deep into the relationship before it is discovered. Keep away from all manner of covert actions and tendencies. They are breeding grounds for the little foxes that ravage the vineyard of relationships.

2. Mutual Respect

Do nothing out of selfish ambition or vain conceit, but in humility consider others better than yourselves.
(Philippians 2:3)

There is something about respect that brings out the self-worth of a person. You must respect each other and also have respect for the choices, values, and goals of the other person even if you do not agree with them. You can disagree without being disagreeable, unless it comes to the question of sin or sinful compromise. But again even here you can disagree without being disrespectful of the person's choices and values. There is respect for a persons' personality. There is respect for a person's values. There is respect for a person's interests. There is respect for a person's choices. And most often you cannot separate the respect you have for a person from that you have for his values, choices or goals. Actually respect has to do with necessary protocol, attitude and manner of speaking. If folks will learn to respect each other, work will be a lot smoother. There are some who think they should be respected by everybody but they make no effort or let alone have respect for the very people from whom they demand respect. Respect is earned rather than demanded. In fact, it is your actions and attitudes that will make others respect you or not. Your degree of respect cannot be higher than your degree of rectitude. In relating with others in spite of their age group or status in society, it is your heart's attitude and actions towards them that will inspire them to respect you. It is not just your title that will bring you respect but your character. That is why the apostle Paul insisted on the fact that someone in a position of spiritual authority must be above reproach (1Timothy 3:2; Titus 1:7). It is the way you live and behave among those you relate with that will earn you their respect. Paul told Timothy to *"set an example for the believers in speech, in life, in love, in faith and in purity"* (1Timothy 4:12), so that no one will look down on him. It is the kind of words you use that will earn you respect. It is your manner of life that will earn you respect. And it is the love you show others that will earn you their respect. So instead of demanding that you be respected, do the things that will win the respect of the people you relate with. When you respect others they in turn will respect you and this will keep your relationship going. You should know that everybody has a right to his or her own opinion. And your own opinion might seem to be the best only to you. Have respect for the ideas, suggestions and viewpoints of others even if you do not buy them. What matters is your attitude!

3. Mutual Identification

15 Rejoice with those who rejoice; mourn with those who mourn. *16* Live in harmony with one another. Do not be proud, but be willing to associate with people of low position. Do not be conceited.

(Romans 12:15 -16)

You must be willing to identify with the other person for the relationship to be sustained. Identify with his strength and weaknesses. Identify with his or her joys and sorrows, successes or failures, gains or losses, in poverty or riches. Permit me to tell you that there is power in mutual identification. Listen, if there must be harmony and unity in any relationship those involved must be committed to mutual identification one with another. This tells the other *"I am with you whatever the situation"*. There are people who do not want to identify themselves with those they relate with. In such a case the relationship cannot be described as sustainable. What makes our relationship with the Lord strong is that He identifies Himself with us. By taking the form of a simple man He demonstrated the ultimate identification. And as we walk on with Him He continues to identify Himself with us in our weaknesses. That is why we want to stick with Him forever. When you identify with others in their time of strength and weakness, health and sickness, joy and pain, success and failure, it adds value to the relationship.

One criterion that will be used on judgement day will be that of identification especially with those in need (see Matthew 25:31–46). When Job was in trouble, his friends, though they had misunderstood the cause of his trials, they however identified with Job when everyone had abandoned him. The Bible lets us to know that those three friends of his left their homes, businesses and whatever else they were doing to come spend time with Job in his state of rejection. They identified themselves with him in his time of trial. Many people today are not committed to this kind of relationship in which they can be counted upon in time of need. Relationships get severed because one or the other fails to identify with the other in time of distress. Some people quickly abandon their friends when they fail. When you identify with someone even when the person has done the worst and he is considered by all as the devil, it will go the whole way to add value to your relationship. Do not be one who is only interested in fair weather relationships. Identifying with someone means standing with them through thick and thin, fair weather or stormy times. There is power in mutual identification to keep a relationship alive, strong and vibrant.

SUMMARY OF THE CHAPTER

- *By transparency, I mean the capacity to be open to each other about your failures and weaknesses.*

- *There is healing power locked up in transparency. When you are open one to the other, wounds will easily be healed. Hurts will be dealt with appropriately.*

- *When you allow doubt to accumulate because you do not ask the right questions, it will definitely insulate and isolate you from each other, thereby weakening the relationship.*

- *Any relationship built on a false impression comes to an abrupt end when the hypocrite is discovered. Even if it does not end abruptly it will inevitable suffer a fatal blow from which it might never recover, but for a supernatural intervention.*

- *Keep away from all manner of covert actions and tendencies. They are breeding grounds for the little foxes that ravage the vineyard of relationships.*

- *You must respect each other and also have respect for the choices, values, and goals of the other person even if you do not agree with them.*

- *You cannot separate the respect you have for a person from that you have for his values, choices or goals.*

- *It is your actions and attitudes that will make others respect you or not. Your degree of respect cannot be higher than your degree of rectitude.*
- *Have respect for the ideas, suggestions and viewpoints of others even if you do not buy them. What matters is your attitude!*
- *If there must be harmony and unity in any relationship those involved must be committed to mutual identification one with another.*
- *What makes our relationship with the Lord strong is that He identifies Himself with us. By taking the form of simple man He demonstrated the ultimate identification.*
- *Relationships get severed because one or the other fails to identify with the other in time of distress.*
- *Do not be one who is only interested in fair weather relationships. Identifying with someone means standing with them through thick and thin, fair weather or stormy times.*

A Friendship Kind of Relationship – 3

1. Mutual Submission

Submit to one another out of reverence for Christ.
(Ephesians 5:21)

For a relationship to be sustained you must submit one to the other. Do not always demand your own way. Be willing to adjust in a way that will show consideration for the other person's opinion, choices, and values. In this way one person does not appear as the boss and the other person the servant whose only response is *"yes sir"*. There is no friendship which can be maintained on the basis of a one-sided *"yes sir"*. You see, mutual submission is very easy when one has come to the point where he or she knows that no one always has the best idea. When you acknowledge the fact that we need each other then it will be easy to submit. Paul said, *"I myself am convinced, my brothers that you* *yourselves are full of goodness, complete in knowledge and <u>competent to instruct one another</u>"* (Romans 15:14, emphasis mine). Everybody has something to contribute. Just lending a listening ear is an act of submission. Accepting someone else's opinion and putting aside yours is an act of submission. For some, submission will mean receiving orders and executing them without raising questions. For others, submission will simply mean to listen to another person. Whatever submission may imply in any given situation, we all need to submit one to the other. It will inspire loyalty, increase output and strengthen the relational connection. If submission is one-sided, the relationship becomes strained and one party becomes defeated in the relationship. Once one party feels defeated, output is reduced. There is a way you can reject someone's opinion without making the person himself feel inferior to you. There are some who get into relationships with others with an air of superiority such that they think that they have all the knowledge and wisdom there is on planet earth. This is detrimental to the relationship. A *"know it all"* attitude will not only strain the relationship but will eventually kill it. It is not a weakness to keep aside your own ideas and ways of doing things to adopt a better one even if it may come from someone you consider inferior whether in education, social or spiritual status. Did you know that there is greatness in submission? It is little men and women who usually feel too big to submit to others. Such always demand absolute submission by others but will never submit or at best, do so grudgingly. Submit to one another and keep your relationship strong.

2. Mutual Forgiveness

Be kind and compassionate to one another, forgiving each other, just as in Christ God forgave you.
(Ephesians 4:32)

Bear with each other and forgive whatever grievances you may have against one another. Forgive as the Lord forgave you.
(Colossians 3:13)

Nobody is perfect. As human beings we are bound to make mistakes and hurt each other even in cases where we think we have taken greatest precaution. No matter how well you select your words there are times when even smooth and well intended words will hurt and wound. For a relationship to be sustained there must be willingness on both sides to forgive even the gravest offence. Nobody who has not learned how to forgive can build any sustainable relationship. It is forgiveness that brings about healing and restoration. You must forgive even if the other party has not seen the wrong he or she has done. Also, transparency will mean you open up and tell the other the way you feel. But you must forgive. When forgiveness is lacking in a relationship, fellowship is naturally hampered no matter how those involved may pretend. Some people think that is pays to hold grudges. Every grudge will eventually develop into ill feelings towards those it is harboured against. One who does not forgive easily will eventually create open doors to spirits of unforgiveness, hate and anger. I was ministering deliverance to a young woman and there was this demon of anger which refused to leave. It claimed that it had a legal ground to be there because this young lady had not forgiven somebody. At a certain point it became so violent that it took Holy Sprit inspired boldness and courage to continue the deliverance session. I had to resort to total warfare to bring the lady back to herself in order to continue her deliverance. You see the spirit understood what the Bible says about unforgiveness. All other spirits fled but it held on because of the legal ground it had. Matthew 18:21–35 shows us the danger of unforgiveness. When you refuse to forgive, you are the first person to suffer. You block your relationship with God and bar the way to your own forgiveness from God (Mathew 6:14-15).

On the other hand, when you forgive someone for a wrong done you give the person the opportunity to improve and to trust you more. The one whom you forgive will be open to confess his or her failures, even ones you may not be aware of because he or she knows that mercy will eventually triumph over judgement. When people relate and operate in an environment in which they know that they can easily be forgiven, they will function effectively. Mutual forgiveness is a vital element in the building of sustainable relationships. Explore it.

3. Mutual Encouragement

Therefore encourage each other with these words.
(1 Thessalonicians 4:18)

Therefore encourage one another and build each other up, just as in fact you are doing.
(1 Thessalonicians 5:11)

To sustain your relationship, learn to be appreciative and to encourage each other. When there is mutual appreciation there will be mutual encouragement. Do not spend your time criticizing each other. It will destroy the relationship. You can critique each other and help each other improve. Encourage each other in their goals and aspirations. This will go a long way to make your relationship strong and productive. It will bring out the best in you. Look for things in and about the other you can appreciate. Another way to be appreciative is to express gratitude for little favours and services rendered. Such shows of gratitude are sure to build the morale of the one being appreciated. Of course high morale will lead to increased output, and by extension a healthier relationship.

I want you to look at the Songs of Solomon. Throughout the book, words of appreciation are mutually exchanged. You must understand that everyone needs encouragement to function well and be at his or her best. Think about it; God asked the prophet Moses more than once to encourage Joshua who was to be his successor in leading the children of Israel in the conquest of the Promise Land (Deuteronomy 1:38; 3:28). You see, even the wicked understand the power of mutual encouragement and make use of it. About them, the psalmist said, *"they encourage each other in evil plans..."* (Psalm 64:5). Encouragement is very vital. It is for this very reason that God decided to raise people in the church whose only gift is that of encouraging the saints in their walk with God (Romans 12:8). Encouragement is something you can, and should, do daily. It is not and isn't supposed to be some occasional thing that you do once in a blue moon. The Bible says,

> But encourage one another daily, as long as it is called Today, so that none of you may be hardened by sin's deceitfulness. (Hebrews 3:13)

"Let us not give up meeting together, as some are in the habit of doing, but let us encourage one another--and all the more as you see the Day approaching" (Hebrews 10:25). God does not attach importance to unimportant things. The fact that the Bible is full of words of encouragement is an indication that we all need it to function at

optimum productivity. There are several ways through which you can encourage someone. I talked already of being appreciative of things in the person's life or about the person and being grateful for little services rendered or favors shown. You can do this using direct words, little notes and gifts to the person. You can take out time to assist the person in whatever he or she is doing. Mutual encouragement is necessary and indispensable for a relationship to be sustainable. Words are such a powerful tool in the business of encouragement. Mastering the right words and using them appropriately will help sustain your relationship.

4. Mutual Understanding

> A man who lacks judgment derides his neighbor, but a man of understanding holds his tongue.
> (Proverb 11:12)

> Understanding is a fountain of life to those who have it, but folly brings punishment to fools.
> (Proverb 16:22)

> By wisdom a house is built, and through understanding it is established.
> (Proverb 24:3)

This is another vital and indispensable element for a sustainable relationship. You can only go with each other as far as you understand each other. Understanding is what will enable you to properly interpret the actions, attitudes and words of the other person. Another cankerworm that ruins relationships is misinterpretation. When you understand each other you will know what the other needs or does not need. Whether he or she wants to be alone or needs your company. Understanding gives you access even to the unspoken words of the other and enables you to make necessary adjustments. If I understand what offends my friend, I will do everything in my power to avoid deliberately offending him. If I understand my friend's temperaments and behavioural patterns, then I will automatically know what approach to use when our friendship is faced with different challenges. Understanding will give you knowledge of how to please your friend. Look at what Proverbs 11:12 says and you will acknowledge that understanding is what will help you choose the right words and speak in the right tone. You won't have to run your mouth when you have understanding. Understanding will be a source of life to the relationship. If your relationship has understanding in it then it will never die because *"understanding is a fountain of life to those who have it..."* Do you want your relationship to stay alive? Then work at mutual understanding. You might have all the wisdom to build relationships but if you lack understanding, your relationships will not last. Understanding gives your relationship stability. From Proverbs 24:3, we see that a relationship is established through understanding. When something is established it means it is made firm, stable and secure. Therefore understanding is what will keep your relationship stable and secure when the storms come raging. A relationship that is lacking in mutual understanding is open to all kinds of predatory vices. Understanding does not just come through your desire for it. You've got to find out what the person likes and dislikes, what pleases or displeases him or her. You know, it is a whole school which will require time and commitment. If you are willing and ready to spend quality time in formal and informal activities, your understanding for each other will be enhanced. Be willing to pay the price to understand those you are relating with if the relationship must stand the test of time and adverse circumstances.

5. Mutual Devotion

> Be devoted to one another in brotherly love. Honor one another above yourselves.
> (Romans 12:10)

Fellowship is the lifeline of every relationship. Where it is absent the relationship is as good as dead. However, unless there is devotion there can be no fellowship. Another thing that easily kills relationship is the lack of devotion. Devotion is the channel through which fellowship flows. Mutual devotion will help you share your resources with each other, be it time, money, possessions, talents or gifts. Mutual devotion will enable you to delight in sacrificing for the other as the need arises. When you are devoted to someone, you will always protect that person and support him or her at all times. Devotion implies loyalty, availability and support. Devotion says *"I am one with you come what may"*. Devotion means love and fidelity. The Bible says, *"A despairing man should have the devotion of his friends, even though he forsakes the fear of the Almighty"* (Job 6:14). Devotion demands dependability. It is very frustrating to be in a relationship, yet be unable to depend on that person when the need arises. Some people act as though they are around only for you to need them and they are nowhere to be found. This betrays their lack of devotion. If a relationship must be sustained, it must have as a vital element the aspect of devotion. Nevertheless, devotion comes as a result of heart fusion and blending. You cannot be devoted to someone with whom your heart has not blended. The thing with many a relationship today is that too many people are involved in building superficial relationships which amount to nothing and produce no effect. When you are devoted to somebody you will have time for the person. You can also make room in your resources no matter how limited they may be in order to accommodate him or her when need be. I have always told my friends that the only thing I cannot do for a friend is that which is absolutely beyond me or that which I do not want to do. I have always found a means to create time for what I want to do. I have always found a means to trim my personal expenses in order to make provisions for someone in need. This is what devotion is all about. Taking risks not because of selfish interest or personal gain but because you are interested in helping someone else who might be in a more precarious situation than you are. Devotion has the power to keep a relationship alive through thick and thin. However, one-sided devotion will not last; it must be mutual.

SUMMARY OF THE CHAPTER

- *Be willing to adjust in a way that will show consideration for the other person's opinion, choices, and values.*
- *Everybody has something to contribute. Just lending a listening ear is an act of submission.*
- *A "know it all" attitude will not only strain the relationship but will eventually kill it.*
- *No matter how well you select your words there are times when even smooth words will hurt and wound.*
- *Nobody who has not learned how to forgive can build any sustainable relationship. It is forgiveness that brings about healing and restoration.*
- *When forgiveness is lacking in a relationship, fellowship is naturally hampered no matter how those involved may pretend.*
- *The individual who does not forgive easily will eventually create open doors to spirits of unforgiveness, hate and anger.*
- *The one whom you forgive will be open to confess his or her failures, even ones you may not be aware of because he or she knows that mercy will eventually triumph over judgment.*

- *When there is mutual appreciation there will be mutual encouragement.*
- *Such shows of gratitude are sure to build the morale of the one being appreciated. Of course high morale will lead to increased output and by extension a healthier relationship.*
- *Words are such a powerful tool in the business of encouragement. Mastering the right words and using them appropriately will help sustain your relationship.*
- *Understanding is what will enable you to properly interpret the actions, attitudes and words of the other person.*
- *If your relationship has understanding in it then it will never die because "understanding is a fountain of life to those who have it..."*
- *Understanding is what will keep your relationship stable and secure when the storms come raging.*
- *If you are willing and ready to spend quality time in formal and informal activities, your understanding for each other will be enhanced.*
- *Devotion is the channel through which fellowship flows. Mutual devotion will help you share your resources with each other, be it time, money, possessions, talents or gifts.*

- *You cannot be devoted to someone with whom your heart has not blended.*
- *I have always told my friends that the only thing I cannot do for a friend is that which is absolutely beyond me or that which I do not want to do.*

Different settings carry with them relationship enhancing elements that are specific to them, but which may not necessarily apply to other settings. In this section, we will look at how we can build sustainable relationships at work and at home.

Chapter Nine

Building Lasting Relationships at the Work Place

1. Be <u>Cognizant</u> of Authority

The first attitude to build in your work place is that of recognition of authority. You will have to first of all identify all those who are above you in the hierarchical order and in what respect you are accountable to them. The Bible says a lot about authority and for you to function efficiently and efficaciously you will have to recognize and be accountable to those who are your superiors. There are many people who have a problem with authority as long as they are not the ones in authority but if they should be in authority, they immediately demand submission from everybody. If you do not respect and obey those over you, no matter how much you labor your labor will not be recognized, let alone appreciated. Like I said before, everyone enjoys being appreciated. Appreciation will boost your morale and increase output.

However, we create a hostile environment when we fail to recognize authority. A hostile environment leads to a lack of appreciation that would inevitably minimize output. When productivity is reduced, it affects our general wellbeing.

> *1* Everyone must submit himself to the governing authorities, for there is no authority except that which God has established. The authorities that exist have been established by God. *2* Consequently, he who rebels against the authority is rebelling against what God has instituted, and those who do so will bring judgment on themselves. *3* For rulers hold no terror for those who do right, but for those who do wrong. Do you want to be free from fear of the one in authority? Then do what is right and he will commend you.
> (Romans 13:1-3)
>
> *13* Submit yourselves for the Lord's sake to every authority instituted among men: whether to the king, as the supreme authority, *14* or to governors, who are sent by him to punish those who do wrong and to commend those who do right
> (1 Peter 2:13-14).

Many conflicts will be resolved if only people would learn to recognize authority wherever they go. Many relationships will be healed, restored, and strengthened. If you do not recognize the authority of someone, there is no way you can enjoy your relationship with the person. Nothing you do can substitute recognizing authority. Let me give you an example from the word. It is the story of Hagar and her mistress Sarah. When Hagar knew she was pregnant for Abraham, she began to despise Sarah's authority, an attitude that made life very difficult for her. She decided to flee from home thinking that the solution was to run away. But the angel of the Lord met her when she was fleeing from home and asked her to return and submit to her mistress. In other words, the angel told Hagar there will be no problem if she would learn to recognize, and be obedient to those in authority over her (see Genesis 16:1-9).

You may be older than the one who is over you; you may have come from a richer home; you may have a better education, but if only you will recognize and obey the one in authority, it will yield you dividends. Learn to recognize authority, make it your goal to do so wherever you go.

2. Be Conscious of your Duties

Duty consciousness is one thing that will help sustain relationships at the place of work. After you have taken cognisance of authority the next thing is naturally to realise what you have to do and do it cheerfully and efficiently. Duty consciousness is encouraged and commanded throughout the Bible. This is because the Lord knows that for the relationship between an employer and an employee to be sustained the one who is employed must be conscious and committed to what he or she is being paid for.

> 5 Slaves, obey your earthly masters with respect and fear, and with sincerity of heart, just as you would obey Christ. 6 Obey them not only to win their favor when their eye is on you, but like slaves of Christ, doing the will of God from your heart. 7 Serve wholeheartedly, as if you were serving the Lord, not men"
> (Ephesians 6:5-7).

The above passage describes the responsibility of both the employer and the employee in building a sustainable relationship. Here, however, our focus at this time is on the role of the employee.

There are many people who are eye servants. They serve when you are around and watching and idle around when your eye is not on them. Such cannot be described as duty conscious. Paul said, *"Whatever you do, work at it with all your heart, as working for the Lord, not for men"* (Colossians 3:23). When the man of God mentions doing something with all your heart, it will require you looking beyond the man to whom you are immediately accountable because you know that, you will also give account to God of that which He entrusted into your hands. Wholehearted commitment to your job will create an environment where your relationship with your boss or employer can be maintained without weakening in its strength or output.

Do you remember what Solomon said? You just have one opportunity to do that which you are doing. And this demands that you do it with all your might. Do not allow the opportunity to pass you by while you indulge in self-sparing. You might live to regret the fact that you never gave it your all. Everybody in his normal senses loves and appreciates the person who works hard. That is why even in a home the parents will appreciate the child who serves at home better than the one who does not. The boss will likewise grant a raise to the one who serves diligently. Some people think because they have served long they are just entitled to a raise. If you have been serving all the time in a self-sparing manner even God will ensure that you are not given a raise. So at the work place, the best you can do for yourself is to be totally committed to what you have been assigned to. This will make things smooth between you and those who matter at your place of work.

3. Be <u>Considerate</u> of your Subordinates

We have written in the last two points about the duties of the subordinates with respect to the boss or employer. For there to be a boss it means there is someone who is answerable to him or her. Now for there to be a sustainable boss-subordinate relationship, just as the subordinate has to be cognizant of authority the boss has to be considerate of his subordinate. There are people who always want to rough-handle those under them. They have no respect for the personality of those they consider their inferiors at the work place. The fact that you are the boss today does not give you the mandate to treat others with disrespect. It does not give you the mandate to look down on them as though they were some nonentities. To be considerate means you treat them as human beings who also have blood running through their veins. They too need appreciation, they want to be valued and treated with dignity. They want to feel needed. If you also let the people who work under you feel that they can be dealt away with at any time, there is no way you can expect them to put in their all and serve wholeheartedly. They will spare some energy to put in some other thing when they are no longer there. Make them feel they are part of what is being done and your relationship with them will be smooth and productive.

> And masters, treat your slaves in the same way. Do not threaten them, since you know that he who is both their Master and yours is in heaven, and there is no favoritism with him.
>
> (Ephesians 6:9)

Here, Paul exhorted the slaves to treat their masters with respect and sincerity of heart and asked that the masters treat their slaves with the same respect and sincerity of heart. He asked them not to threaten their slaves. You see threats have the capacity to reduce one's efficiency and increase insecurity. When you always pronounce threats you make the work place intimidating and uncomfortable for those who are supposed to produce the results. You are the boss because they are there. If no one were under you, you would never be the boss. So treat them as people who have given you the opportunity to be what you are.

> Masters, provide your slaves with what is right and fair, because you know that you also have a Master in heaven.
> (Colossians 4:1)

Another way to be considerate of your subordinates is to provide them with what they need to function well. The guiding rule is to provide them with what is right and fair. Do not expect results for which you have not made provisions. The question you should constantly ask yourself as one in authority is whether you have done all that is necessary for the best results to be produced. What have you provided for those working for you that your competitors have not made available to theirs? What rare privileges do they have that will cause them to function better than everyone else? If you just do what everybody else has done to their worker, then the best they will do is produce like everyone else. Do you know the best way to know what is fair? It is to put yourself in the shoes of others and consider how you would want to be treated. With that in mind, you will get a feel of what to do for those you are supervising.

4. Be Cooperative with Colleagues

We have looked at vertical relationships at the work place. Now let's look at them on the horizontal plane. Not everyone at work is a boss or a subordinate. To make things smooth for you at your place of work, you have to be cooperative with those with whom you are working. Some people are the very architect of their own misery at the place of work because they try to function as an island. You must learn to develop means by which you can reach out to others and be equally accessible to others. When you get to the work place do not wait to be greeted by others; rather, take the initiative to greet your colleagues and find out how they slept and how they woke up. Find out what you can do to be of help to those who are in some kind of need. You can be of help morally, financially, spiritually, and otherwise to people at your place of work. Make the environment around you sociable. Be sure that you are approachable by your colleagues. If you make the environment tense, you will be the first person to suffer isolation. Take the initiative to make little gifts to your colleagues without expecting reciprocity. When you cooperate with colleagues, it will help you function well at your work place as you will not only be making things comfortable for yourself but for others as well. This will create the necessary social climate to enhance efficiency and increase output.

Be willing to share your experiences and expertise with others. When you let others know that you are willing to teach them skills they may not have, they will in turn teach you skills you might not have. You do not know everything. You see, there are people who think that the little knowledge they have is all they need to know. Even if the other person might not teach you things which may be of benefit at the work place, he or she might teach you things that will benefit you out of the place of work. He who thinks he knows everything knows nothing. You can never know it all; the one thing you don't know is what you do not know, so set out to learn. The whole aspect of cooperation with others is a school; you alone will determine how far you will go in the mastery of what you need to learn.

5. Be <u>Calm</u> in all you do

Levelheadedness is indispensable for you to function well and build sustainable relationships at the place of work. There are people who are always tense and make the environment tense. When an environment is tense, the propensity for conflict is very high. The slightest offence or mistake will stir troubled waters that would otherwise have remained calm. You need to be levelheaded at all times at the place of work. One way to ensure that you are always levelheaded is to leave domestic problems at home where they belong. Those you must carry along must end at the gate of your place of work. Those problems out of the work place should not even pay you a visit in the office. If they do, it will destroy the social climate and decrease output. Levelheadedness will enable you speak to others in the right tone. It will make you appreciative instead of being critical. It will make you want to see the best in others and to bring out the best from others. It will make you want to always put in your all and be at your best. When you are tense you function far below your capacity and therefore your output is minimized. Your employer has made your work place comfortable for you; do not allow the intricacies of your personal life to interfere with your work. This amounts to cheating your employer. Remember, no relationship can last when one party feels consistently cheated by the other.

SUMMARY OF THE CHAPTER

- *Identify all those who are above you in the hierarchical order and in what respect you are accountable to them.*
- *If you do not respect and obey those over you, no matter how much you labor your labor will not be recognized, let alone appreciated.*
- *A hostile environment leads to a lack of appreciation that would inevitably minimize output.*
- *Nothing you do can substitute recognizing authority.*
- *After you have taken cognisance of authority the next thing is naturally to realise what you have to do and do it cheerfully and efficiently.*
- *Wholehearted commitment to your job will create an environment where your relationship with your boss or employer can be maintained without weakening in its strength or output.*
- *Do not allow the opportunity to pass you by while you indulge in self-sparing. You might live to regret the fact that you never gave it your all.*
- *At the work place, the best you can do for yourself is to be totally committed to what you have been assigned to.*
- *If you also let the people who work under you feel that they can be dealt away with at any time, there*

is no way you can expect them to put in their all and serve wholeheartedly.

- *When you always pronounce threats you make the work place intimidating and uncomfortable for those who are supposed to produce the results.*

- *If you just do what everybody else has done to their worker, then the best they will do is produce like everyone else.*

- *When you cooperate with colleagues, it will help you function well at your work place as you will not only be making things comfortable for yourself but for others as well.*

- *Be willing to share your experiences and expertise with others. When you let others know that you are willing to teach them skills they may not have, they will in turn teach you skills you might not have.*

- *One way to ensure that you are always levelheaded is to leave domestic problems at home where they belong. Those you must carry along must end at the gate of your place of work. Those problems out of the work place should not even pay you a visit in the office.*

- *Your employer has made your work place comfortable for you; do not allow the intricacies of your personal life to interfere with your work. This amounts to cheating your employer.*

Let's move to another setting of relationships — the home.

Chapter Ten

Building Lasting Relationships at Home

Just as there are different qualities essential to building relationships at work, there are qualities which are essentially particular to building sustainable relationships at home. We are going to look at four underlying qualities.

1. Be Available

One of the most important qualities to build a sustainable relationship at home is the aspect of availability; spouses being available one to the other; being available to the children, children being available to parents and to one another. Availability implies being present and ready for use; being within reach and accessible. It talks of being willing to be of service or assistance as the need arises. Availability will create an atmosphere of trust and security. When people are in an environment where they are sure that when they cry for help there will be someone extending a hand, that when they are lonely there will be someone to keep them company, that when they cry someone will always be there to comfort them, they will be prepared to put in their best for the wellbeing of others. Children should be available to assist their parents in one thing or another. You can assist in cleaning their shoes and ensuring that they are ready when they need them. You can make yourself available to help in the kitchen or anywhere else around the house. Availability enhances cooperation and understanding.

When is someone unavailable?

- When they are always absent.
- When they cannot be reached easily.
- When they are unwilling to be of service or assistance.
- When they are not ready every time they are needed.
- When they have to be called every time there is something to be done.

2. Be Accountable

Accountability is another quality that must exist for there to be healthy relationships in the home. Spouses must be accountable to one another and to their children; children must be accountable to their parents and to one another. Accountability will mean you letting the other members of your household know where you are going to and possibly when you will be back. It will mean you calling the home to tell the others that you will be coming late in cases where you may have to return home later than usual. You can be accountable with respect to financial expenditure. You see children can earn the trust of their parents by being accountable of how they spend the money that is given them. Be accountable to each other about your friendships and other relationships. There is no need to have relationships which you cannot with a free conscious let other members of the home know about. There are people who give the impression that their relationship with someone is casual meanwhile it may be very intimate. Any relationship whose intimacy you are not free to disclose is a questionable one. Be accountable to each other about your transactions. It will create an atmosphere of transparency. By this you will be able to help protect each other from harmful relationships and dangerous ventures. The home is meant to protect members of the home from the wrong kind of people. There is power in accountability. Others can help you discern flaws that you might not be able to see even if you looked at the situation with the eye of an eagle. It gives the others in your household the opportunity to be an integral part of your life.

3. Be Responsible

Responsibility means executing one's duties, fulfilling one's obligations, and bearing one's own share of the burden of the home. Life will be a lot more fulfilling if only the members of a household will take it upon themselves to be responsible. Those who are responsible do not blame others for the things that happen to them; they are willing to find out where they went wrong instead of looking for a scapegoat. Responsibility implies the willingness to bear the consequences of one's own actions without transferring blame or aggression on anyone else. It talks of being reliable and dependable. Members of the household must be able to rely and depend on you within the sphere of that for which you are responsible. Do not wait to be told to do what you already know to do. Do not expect to be begged to assist when there is need. It is all a matter of taking the initiative to do little things that will benefit the home as a whole.

4. Be Respectful

When people in a home have respect for one another, a strong bond will be established between them, hence a sustainable relationship can be built. Respect is all about taking notice of the sacrifices of others and acknowledging that which they do. It is regarding each other with special attention. It is to regard each other as worthy of special consideration. It is all about caring for one another and taking heed to the counsel and suggestions of one another.

SUMMARY OF THE CHAPTER

- *It talks of being willing to be of service or assistance as the need arises. Availability will create an atmosphere of trust and security.*
- *Availability enhances cooperation and understanding.*
- *Accountability will mean you letting the other members of your household know where you are going to and possibly when you will be back. It will mean you calling the home to tell the others that you will be coming late in cases where you may have to return home later than usual.*
- *Others can help you discern flaws that you might not be able to see even if you looked at the situation with the eye of an eagle.*
- *Responsibility implies the willingness to bear the consequences of one's own actions without transferring blame or aggression on anyone else.*
- *Respect is all about taking notice of the sacrifices of others and acknowledging that which they do. It is regarding each other with special attention. It is to regard each other as worthy of special consideration.*

www.ingramcontent.com/pod-product-compliance
Lightning Source LLC
Chambersburg PA
CBHW031253290426
44109CB00012B/555